Euthanasia and the Churches

Christian Ethics in Dialogue Series
Editors: Robin Gill and Wesley Carr

The Cassell Christian Ethics in Dialogue Series is intended for churches, students of ethics, policy makers and Christians in public life. It is designed to address moral dilemmas which have three things in common. First, they are deeply contentious. Then, they stand at the interface between public standards and personal morality. And finally, they are key issues for lawmakers. What a society does about them contributes to the way that society sees itself and—to an extent—to the way the world judges it.

The series, which is ecumenical, will be associated with a programme of international consultations to be held in the Jerusalem Chamber at Westminster Abbey, London. It will involve influential Christians and others from a wide range of contexts and religious backgrounds.

The Series Editors represent two worlds which are pivotal for the thinking and praxis of the churches. From the world of academic theology is Robin Gill, Michael Ramsey Professor of Modern Theology at the University of Kent at Canterbury, currently President of the British Society for the Study of Christian Ethics. From the heart of the public life of the church comes Dr Wesley Carr, Dean of Westminster.

Already published:
Euthanasia and the Churches

Forthcoming titles include:
The Arms Trade
Public Morality, Private Morality

Euthanasia and the Churches

Edited by Robin Gill

CASSELL

Cassell
Wellington House, 125 Strand, London WC2R OBB
370 Lexington Avenue, New York, NY 10017–6550
www.cassell.co.uk

First published 1998

British Library Cataloguing-in-Publication Data
A catalogue record for this book is available from the British Library.

ISBN 0-304-70352-4

Designed by Geoff Green
Typeset by Fakenham Photosetting Limited, Fakenham, Norfolk NR21 8NL
Printed and bound in Great Britain
by Biddles Ltd, Guildford and King's Lynn

Contents

6 *Contents*

Section 3
Euthanasia and the principle of justice

Contributors

Paul Badham is Professor of Theology and Religious Studies at the University of Wales, Lampeter, where he is Director of the MA in Death and Immortality and contributor to the MA in Contemporary Death Studies. His books include *Christian Beliefs About Life After Death* (Macmillan, 1976) and *Immortality or Extinction?* (Macmillan, 1982), and he has edited *Ethics on the Frontiers of Human Existence* (Paragon, 1992) and *Facing Death* (University of Wales Press, 1996).

Nigel Biggar is Fellow and Chaplain of Oriel College, Oxford, where he teaches ethics and systematic theology in the University's Faculty of Theology. His publications include *Good Life: Reflections on What We Value Today* (SPCK, 1997) and *The Hastening That Waits: Karl Barth's Ethics* (Oxford University Press, 1993).

Alastair Campbell is the inaugural Professor of Ethics in Medicine in the School of Medicine, University of Bristol, and Director of the Centre for Ethics in Medicine. Previously he was Associate Dean of the Faculty of Divinity in the University of Edinburgh, Professor of Biomedical Ethics at Otago Medical School, and foundation editor of the *Journal of Medical Ethics*. His books include *Health As Liberation* (Pilgrim Press, 1995) and *Medical Ethics*, co-authored with Max Charlesworth, Grant Gillett and Gareth Jones (Oxford University Press, 1997).

Karen Forbes is Macmillan Consultant Senior Lecturer in Palliative Medicine at the University of Bristol.

Robin Gill is the first Michael Ramsey Professor of Modern Theology at the University of Kent at Canterbury. Previously he was the first William Leech Professorial Fellow at Newcastle University and, earlier, Associate Dean of Divinity at Edinburgh University. His books include *Christian Ethics in Secular Worlds* (T. & T. Clark, 1991), *A Textbook of Christian Ethics* (T. & T. Clark, revised edition 1995) and *Moral Leadership in a Postmodern Age* (T. & T. Clark, 1997).

Peter Howdle is Professor of Clinical Education and Consultant Physician and Gastroenterologist at St James's University Hospital, Leeds. He is responsible for the clinical education of undergraduate medical students at the University of Leeds and serves on a Multi-Centre Research Ethics Committee. He is a Methodist Local Preacher.

Ian Leck is Professor Emeritus and former Professor of Epidemiology at the University of Manchester, and a Methodist Local Preacher. He has served on various bodies concerned with health-care ethics, and gave the 1993 Milroy Lecture of the Royal College of Physicians of London ('Clinical and public health ethics: conflicting or complementary?').

Julie Norris is a Methodist minister with an interest in medical ethics. She taught ethics for Wesley House at Cambridge Federation of Theological Colleges from 1992 to 1996.

Michael Northcott is Senior Lecturer in Christian Ethics and Practical Theology at the University of Edinburgh. Among his publications are *The Church and Secularisation: Urban Industrial Mission in North East England* (Peter Lang, 1989), *The Environment and Christian Ethics* (Cambridge University Press, 1996) and *Urban Theology: A Reader* (Cassell, 1998).

Helen Oppenheimer is a graduate of Lady Margaret Hall, Oxford, (Philosophy, Politics and Economics), and a Lambeth Doctor of

Divinity. From 1965 to 1969 she taught ethics at Cuddesdon Theological College. Her books include *The Hope of Happiness: A Sketch for a Christian Humanism* (SCM Press, 1983) and *Finding and Following: Talking with Children About God* (SCM Press, 1994).

Susan Parsons was Principal, East Midlands Ministry Training Course, Nottingham, and is the author of *Feminism and Christian Ethics* (Cambridge University Press, 1996).

Jean Porter is Professor of Moral Theology at the University of Notre Dame. Previously she taught at Vanderbilt Divinity School. Her publications include *The Recovery of Virtue* (Westminster/John Knox Press, 1990) and *Moral Action and Christian Ethics* (Cambridge University Press, 1995).

Patrick Richmond is curate at the Church of the Martyrs, Leicester. He read medicine at Balliol College, Oxford and, after doing a doctorate in physiology there, he spent six months in Pakistan working with heroin addicts. He returned to Oxford to train at Wycliffe Hall.

Preface

The issue of euthanasia is being widely debated in many countries. It has been the subject of several government reports and is frequently discussed in the media. Yet there has been relatively little debate about it within the Churches. Perhaps it is simply assumed that most Christians are united in their opposition to assisted suicide and voluntary euthanasia (terms which are defined in this volume), so there is little to discuss.

Such a view is only possible if the voices of lay Christians are ignored. Evidence presented in this volume suggests that many regular churchgoers—perhaps even a majority in some countries—apparently agree with legalizing some forms of active euthanasia. Whereas most theologians and church leaders have remained opposed, many lay Christians appear not to be. Some of the articles that follow will examine this dichotomy. For the moment it surely points to the need for a more public debate about euthanasia within the Churches. This book is designed to stimulate that debate.

The format is experimental and was suggested in the first place by the *Epworth Review*. The editor, Dr Richard Jones, wrote suggesting it to me after he had read a copy of my paper which was first delivered as a lecture for the Guild of St Raphael. This paper, the three responses and my reply were then published in the *Epworth Review*. I am most grateful to Dr Jones for allowing me to reproduce them again here and to copy the idea for the papers by

Professor Paul Badham and Professor Alastair Campbell. An
earlier version of Paul Badham's paper first appeared in *Studies in
Christian Ethics*. A crucial section on procedural deterioration has
been added to it. Nonetheless I am most grateful to Dr Linda
Woodhead, the editor, for allowing me to reproduce parts of the
earlier article.

The pattern of article, responses and reply has been comple-
mented by a final overview by Professor Jean Porter. This is
especially useful as she is a distinguished American moral theologian who also knows the British debate well. I must be careful not
to add yet another level of comment in this Preface. However, I am
most grateful to her for taking the trouble to read the debate within
the text carefully and then to respond herself.

Manifestly this debate will continue to divide Christians. Yet I
hope that this book will help us to understand our differences a
little more clearly and, perhaps, sympathetically. The general level
of courtesy in the responses and replies is surely encouraging.

I hope that this book will inspire an ethics in dialogue in other
areas of current Christian concern, perhaps using the experimental format adopted here. I believe that we do need to have such
debates.

Robin Gill

Section 1

The challenge of euthanasia

ROBIN GILL

How should Christians respond to increasing calls in many parts of the world for the legalization of euthanasia? In the Netherlands euthanasia is now *de facto* legal, and only some Churches there have been hostile to this. The agreement of the judiciary there not to prosecute doctors, provided they comply with official guidelines, has allowed the widespread use of euthanasia for terminally ill patients whether they are conscious or not. In Australia's Northern Territory's legislation, which was strongly opposed by a number of church leaders, three patients were assisted to suicide until the decision was overturned by the Federal Parliament. And in the United States, despite the Supreme Court decision of July 1997 not to make illegal State laws prohibiting euthanasia, local courts have so far failed to convict Dr Jack Kevorkian for his open involvement in assisted suicide. Even in Britain it is now clear that the 1994 House of Lords Select Committee's *Report on Medical Ethics*—which argued decisively against legalized euthanasia; and on which the then Archbishop of York, John Habgood, served—has not ended the debate.

Until recently most church leaders and theologians agreed that both assisted suicide and active euthanasia were wrong and should not be condoned or legalized.[1] They often argued that there were ambiguous situations in which the terminally ill could be given pain relief that might or might not shorten their lives. There were also other situations in which competent patients who were

terminally ill might properly decide for themselves against any further life-sustaining treatment. However, it was often argued that
neither of these situations should be termed 'euthanasia' as such.
The latter involved active intervention by medical staff specifically
intended to end a patient's life. Such intervention might take the
form of assisted suicide in which medical staff help a patient to end
his or her life. Or it might take the more active form of medical staff
themselves ending the life of a compliant or comatose patient. In
either case, medical staff would be doing more than agreeing not
to treat, or treating only with the specific intention of controlling
pain. Euthanasia in this strict sense involves medical assistance to,
or action on, a patient with the intention of ending a human life. It
will be seen later that this strict definition still has problems—not
least in the ever more complex medical area of withholding or
withdrawing treatment from the permanently comatose. But for
the moment 'medical assistance or action which is intended to end
a human life' does at least provide a working definition of euthanasia in its strictest sense.

Euthanasia defined in this sense has obvious continuities with
medically induced abortion. Insofar as a foetus constitutes human
life in some sense, medically induced abortion involves assistance
or action which is intended to end a life. Both euthanasia and abortion are contrary to the Hippocratic Oath in its original form. There
is, of course, considerable and probably unresolvable debate about
the status of life of the foetus. Some hold that from conception this
is a full human being who must be accorded full human rights
and/or respect. Others argue that at most it is potential human life
over which the rights or even concerns of the mother should
always be allowed to prevail. However, whichever moral perspective or variant on these perspectives is taken, induced abortion does
entail action which is intended to end a life. And the nearer to term
that this action takes place, the more people whatever their perspective are likely to see abortion as approximating to euthanasia.
Thus the recent debate in the United States about what are sometimes termed partial-birth abortions has highlighted just how
narrow is the distinction between such late-term abortion and

infanticide. Indeed some people, such as the secular philosopher Peter Singer, argue that if abortion is permitted then so should infanticide.[2] A severely malformed baby might even be accorded fewer rights than a higher primate. And just as malformed babies might legitimately be killed, so might permanently comatose adults or the terminally ill who wished to die. Given current advances in the care of premature births, third trimester abortions have many of the features of euthanasia in the strict sense defined above.

Though there has been a long history of theological and pastoral differences within the Churches on the propriety of early abortions, there is a more consistent tradition of condemning most late abortions, infanticide and suicide as sinful. Certainly for Augustine, all would have been seen as murder and as theologically unjustifiable forms of human killing. In *The City of God* he even condemned the notion of altruistic suicide. Medically assisted suicide of the terminally ill would surely have been even less likely to have met with his approval. Thus he argued:

Some women killed themselves to avoid suffering anything [like rape] and surely any man of compassion would be ready to excuse the emotions which led them to do this. Some refused to kill themselves, because they did not want to escape another's criminal act by a misdeed of their own. And anyone who uses this as a charge against them will lay himself open to a charge of foolishness. For it is clear that if no one has a private right to kill even a guilty man (and no law allows this), then certainly anyone who kills himself is a murderer, and is the more guilty in killing himself the more innocent he is of the charge on which he has condemned himself to death. We rightly abominate the act of Judas, and the judgment of truth is that when he hanged himself he did not atone for the guilt of his detestable betrayal but rather increased it, since he despaired of God's mercy and in a fit of self-destructive remorse left himself no chance of a saving repentance. How much less right has anyone to indulge in self-slaughter when he can find in himself no fault to justify such a punishment! For when Judas killed himself, he killed a criminal, and yet he ended his life guilty not only of Christ's death, but also of his own; one crime led to another. Why then should a man, who has done no wrong, do wrong to himself? Why should he kill the innocent in putting himself to death, to prevent a guilty man from doing it? Why should he commit a sin against himself to deprive someone else of the chance?[3]

For Augustine human killing was only justified if it was done under authority. The apparent suicide of Samson, for example, when he pulled down the temple on himself and others was finally justified for Augustine by the belief that God had ordered him to do this. If Samson had simply decided to do this for himself, it would never have been justifiable, however worthy his intentions. Rather, it was justifiable for Augustine because he believed that Samson acted on the authority of God.

Interestingly, it is possible to argue on Augustine's grounds that if euthanasia were legalized by a particular State then it would be justifiable for doctors within that State to practise it. Strictly speaking, they would be acting under the authority of the State and not on their own authority. Unlike Tertullian, who abhorred human killing in any form, Augustine was prepared to sanction capital punishment and State wars provided that they were properly authorized. Of course, viewed from a late-twentieth-century perspective his notion of authority appears dangerously unconditional here. It provides few of the safeguards against unjust laws, coercive States and theocratic claims that have marred so much Christian history. Yet it proved an important stepping-stone in making later distinctions between just and unjust wars, and between killing and murder.

Apart from the issue of early abortion, the Christian tradition condemning medical assistance or action which is intended to end a human life has until recently seldom been challenged by theologians. Earlier this century a few church leaders in Britain such as Dean Inge and W. R. Matthews did challenge it, as did the theologian Joseph Fletcher in the United States. They were exceptions however. For most church leaders and theologians the tradition was intact and voices challenging it either inside the Churches or outside were unusual. It was widely argued that it was not a proper or appropriate role for medical staff to end human life which had been given and sanctified by God. The proper role for medical staff was to save life and not to destroy it.

Given this understanding, the legalization of abortion in 1968 represented a radical shift of medical ethos. It has continued to cause controversy within the Churches and is a source of ongoing theological disagreement. Now it seems likely that euthanasia will create similar divisions. The Christian tradition condemning medical assistance or action which is intended to end a human life is likely to come under increasing challenge within Churches and among theologians. If this was once a debate between Christians and secularists, it is fast becoming a debate among and between Christians. There are at least three reasons for this: changing attitudes within society at large which increasingly affect churchgoers; ambiguities arising from ever more complex medical technology; and finally ambiguities inherent within theology itself. However, there is a fourth factor—ambiguities in legislation—which may pull in the opposite direction.

Changing attitudes

One of the factors which prompted the legalization of abortion in Britain was a change in public opinion. Doubtless this was in turn shaped by such factors as evidence about the prevalence of illegal and particularly septic abortions. Whatever the reasons for the change, by the mid-1980s there was widespread support for abortion, especially in those cases where the woman's health was endangered, where the woman had been raped, or where there was a defect in the embryo. What is more, regular churchgoers also tended to support abortion in such cases. Sharp differences between churchgoers and non-churchgoers emerged only in cases of abortion where the couple reported that they could not afford to have a baby or where the woman simply said that she did not wish to have a child. And even then, there was a minority of regular churchgoers, even among Roman Catholics, who supported abortion on grounds of finance or choice.

Data which I have analysed from *British Social Attitudes*[4] surveys, 1983–87 combined, give a very clear insight into these changing attitudes and the way they affect regular churchgoers. Asked whether or not abortion should be allowed on the grounds of the woman's health being endangered, 92 per cent of Anglican weekly churchgoers thought that it should, as did 65 per cent of Roman Catholic weekly churchgoers; while 88 per cent of Anglican and 63 per cent of Roman Catholic weekly churchgoers thought that abortion should be allowed on grounds of rape (among Roman Catholic monthly churchgoers, this rose to 81 per cent). The Church of England's Board of Social Responsibility report *Abortion: An Ethical Discussion* argued in 1965 against defective embryos being allowed as a legal ground for abortion. This distinguished report argued that such a ground would further disadvantage the disabled and offered a less than Christian understanding of what it is to be a person. However, in the BSA surveys two decades later, 82 per cent of Anglican weekly churchgoers now supported abortion in such cases. Roman Catholic weekly churchgoers at 43 per cent were distinctly less supportive, but among their monthly churchgoers this rose to 76 per cent.

This is not to argue that churchgoers simply mirror the views of secular society in this area. Very clear and statistically significant differences emerged on financial and pro-choice grounds for abortion. Whereas 55 per cent of nominal Anglicans who never went to church supported abortion on purely financial grounds and 45 per cent on pro-choice grounds, among weekly churchgoers this reduced to 30 per cent and 25 per cent respectively. Among Roman Catholic weekly churchgoers support reduced still further to 15 per cent and 12 per cent respectively. So on these two grounds— financial and pro-choice—churchgoers on average were different from non-churchgoers. Yet this was not an absolute difference. More than a fifth of weekly churchgoers across denominations and more than a third of monthly churchgoers supported abortion even on these two grounds. Conversely about a half of the non-churchgoers did not give positive support for such abortions.

A very similar pattern among churchgoers and between churchgoers and non-churchgoers now seems to be emerging on the issue of euthanasia. There is increasing evidence for popular support of euthanasia in certain circumstances, even among regular churchgoers. Again using data which I have analysed from *British Social Attitudes* surveys, this time 1983–84 combined, the following pattern emerges. Most people, including many churchgoers, support changes in the law which would allow euthanasia or assisted suicide for the terminally ill. Conversely, few people support the legalization of euthanasia simply for those who are tired of living but are not terminally ill. There are clear differences between churchgoers and non-churchgoers in this area, yet they are by no means absolute differences. Of the whole 1983–84 sample, 76 per cent were in favour of euthanasia being allowed for the terminally ill, but by 1994 this had risen to 82 per cent. Support among monthly churchgoers across denominations in these two decades differed little from the sample as a whole—72 per cent and 84 per cent respectively. It was only among weekly churchgoers that a statistically significant difference emerged, with support at 48 per cent and 45 per cent respectively. Among Anglican weekly churchgoers in 1983–84 support rose to 66 per cent. The clearest opposition to this form of euthanasia was among Roman Catholic weekly churchgoers: here only 39 per cent supported it, although among monthly attenders this rose to 75 per cent. Among the 1983–84 weekly churchgoers across denominations, age was not a strong predictor of attitudes: 47 per cent of those aged 18–39 and 51 per cent of those aged 60 or over expressed support for euthanasia for the terminally ill.

In 1994 BSA asked people whether they thought that the law should let close relatives assist the suicide of the terminally ill: 54 per cent of the sample as a whole agreed that it should. Again only 25 per cent of weekly churchgoers agreed, yet among monthly churchgoers this rose to 52 per cent. Directional statistical analysis on this and the previous question does suggest that the more an individual goes to church the less likely she or he is to accept the legalization of euthanasia or assisted suicide. None the less, there is still a clear minority of weekly churchgoers who do accept such legislation and a clear minority of non-churchgoers who do not. Even the 1983–84 question about allowing for euthanasia for those who are simply tired of living showed that 6 per cent of weekly churchgoers, as distinct from 12 per cent of the sample as a whole, agreed to this.

It is still too early to analyse the very detailed questions asked about euthanasia in the 1995 BSA survey.[5] For the first time this survey asked people to make judgements about eight different euthanasia scenarios, ranging from euthanasia for the permanently comatose to assisted suicide for those who are simply tired of living. Once again it suggests strong popular support for medically administered euthanasia for the terminally ill, together with a fairly nuanced understanding of differences between the scenarios. People do seem prepared to make distinctions and do not give undifferentiated support for euthanasia in any form. So there appears to be strong support for euthanasia/assisted suicide for those who are terminally ill, but little for those who are not but are simply tired of living. There is also strong support for withdrawing life support from the permanently comatose. In addition, church-going appears to be a highly significant variable in predicting attitudes towards euthanasia. Indeed, regular attendance at a place of worship seems to be a more significant variable than age, gender or social class. So, combining all the different scenarios, weekly churchgoers have a rating of 3.95 on an eight-point scale (i.e. just less than half support the different forms of euthanasia) whereas non-churchgoers have a rating of 5.08, and those saying they have no religion 5.53.

It is often argued that Christian ethics cannot be shaped by opinion polls. Yet, since these data give evidence about the attitudes of regular churchgoers, it might seem less than prudent for Christian ethicists simply to ignore them. Churchgoing does appear to modify support for euthanasia. Those, like myself, who are cautious about supporting any legislation allowing euthanasia can draw some comfort from these statistics. Nevertheless, there is also clear evidence, especially among Anglican regular churchgoers, that a majority of the laity do seem to support change, at least for the terminally ill.

Changes in medicine

The second factor which challenges traditional Christian condemnation of euthanasia is medicine itself. In the public's mind, modern medicine may have become too efficient at saving and pro-longing life. The opinion poll data suggest strongly that there is widespread popular support among both churchgoers and non-churchgoers for medical assistance or action which is intended to end the life of a terminally ill patient. This is not indiscriminate support based upon an unqualified pro-choice perspective. There appears to be little public support for allowing euthanasia for the non-terminally ill who are simply tired of life. And there is some hesitation about allowing close relatives to take the lives of even the terminally ill. Yet there does seem to be a belief that medical staff should be allowed actively to end the lives of both the ter-minally ill who desire this for themselves, and the permanently comatose whose relatives agree. This belief may well be based upon a fear that modern medicine has become too clever at preserving life.

Many people apparently fear that their lives will be inappropri-ately prolonged by the increasing sophistications of modern med-icine. The widespread publicity given to the Tony Bland case may well have added to this fear. Newspapers gave considerable space in the early 1990s to the efforts of his parents to have his life support removed. The House of Lords judgment of 3 February 1993 finally allowed for this to happen and, thus, for Tony Bland to die. The case served to highlight some of the complexities created by advances in medical care. Apparently, patients lacking any cortical activity— and thus without any ability to be sentient or conscious, let alone relate to other people—might have their lives prolonged for years if not for decades. Newspaper photographs of Tony Bland still in a foetal position three-and-a-half years after the Hillsborough dis-aster illustrated this graphically. The House of Lords' *Report on Medical Ethics* pointed out that few of the public when questioned wished to be kept alive in such a state themselves. The 1995 BSA data confirm this.

It is sometimes argued that other advances in modern medicine, particularly in palliative care, work in the opposite direction. For example, the House of Lords' *Report on Medical Ethics* noted that palliative care is not well developed in the Netherlands and argued that the legalization of euthanasia in Britain might erode its impact here. This is an important point, but I doubt if it fully answers the widespread fear of both churchgoers and non-churchgoers. The fear may not simply be about facing intractable pain (an obvious concern for the conscious terminally ill) but about facing prolonged insentience. Involved in this are more complex issues of dignity, identity, and being an unnecessary burden upon others.

Changes in theology

This cluster of complex issues—dignity, identity and burden—raises the issue of euthanasia in a new form for theology. It might in the past have been sufficient simply to argue that human life is God-given and should never be taken by human beings outside the context of just war or just punishment. However, the dilemmas created by modern medicine seem to make such a clear-cut position increasingly difficult to hold. Is withdrawing life-sustaining medical treatment or intensive nursing care from a patient whose cortex is destroyed tantamount to euthanasia or not? Is withholding life-prolonging treatment with the agreement of conscious but terminally ill patients tantamount to assisted suicide or not? Modern medicine makes such questions unavoidable. Fine but apparently arbitrary distinctions need to be made to answer these questions—distinctions which seem to provide a less than firm foundation for theology in this area.

The 1996 *Washington Report* is remarkable because it takes seriously the role of theology, the complexities of the present medical situation, and the ambiguities of law-making in this area. The authors are agreed that if euthanasia/assisted suicide is to be allowed at all then it should be allowed only for exceptional cases of terminal illness. However, they fail finally to agree about whether or not even this should be allowed. Instead, they note the following theological paradox:

Paradoxically, those Christians who accept and those who reject assisted suicide and euthanasia begin with similar convictions. Both have a sense

of the sovereignty of God. Both want to protect human dignity and to preserve the freedom of individual persons to choose how to confront human
finitude and death. They both view life as a gift that is good, but not
entirely at the disposal of humanity ... They recognize that human life,
especially in situations of death and dying, often confronts us with a conflict of goods in which physical life clashes with other purposes or goods of
life. Moreover, they are aware that advances in medical technology may be
used to preserve and extend life apart from other goods of human life. They
agree that the goals of medicine include the relief of suffering and the restoration of health, not simply the extension of physical life.[6]

This provides the third plank for my argument, namely that the
Christian tradition condemning medical assistance or action
which is intended to end a human life is likely to come under
increasing challenge within churches and among theologians. A
single example might illustrate this point. It is often argued by
theologians in this context that human life is a gift, a gift from a
loving God made known to us in Jesus Christ. The analogy of the
gift relationship finds its foundation in God's gift of Jesus Christ as
the Logos and continues in the Logos' gift of life to us. We, in turn,
should respond to this gift with gratitude, thanksgiving and deep
responsibility. In contrast, those who lack this faith may see
human life not as a gracious gift, but as a chance by-product of a
world that has meaning only if we choose to give it meaning. In
theory at least, this second position allows human beings to shape
human life as they will. If people decide to opt for euthanasia then
that is their choice: life can be shaped by their will. Conversely, for
Christians, life is God-given and is not simply to be shaped by the
will of humans, but is to be approached gratefully and responsibly.

Yet in the context of modern medicine the contrast between
these two positions is not nearly so clear-cut. Christian doctors,
committed to the belief that life is God-given, still face the same
dilemmas about prolonging the lives of the terminally ill or permanently comatose. Gift relationships are by no means all gracious—some can be highly manipulative, especially the required
gifts of submission. Gracious gifts should be treated with gratitude
and responsibility, but they should not bind the one to whom they
are given—it is manipulative gifts that do that. Gracious gifts can

be enjoyed for a while and then shared with, or even returned with gratitude to, the giver. Gracious gifts leave both giver and receiver free. Indeed when God-given life becomes nothing but a burden, it might seem appropriate to return that life prayerfully and humbly to the giver.

Changes in law

Taken together, changing attitudes within society which increasingly affect churchgoers, ambiguities arising from ever more complex medical technology, and finally ambiguities inherent within theology itself, seem to make traditional Christian teaching about euthanasia less convincing today. Does this mean that Christians should support a change in legislation about euthanasia/assisted suicide? Clearly, quite a number of churchgoers already believe that it does. My own position is more cautious. If the 1968 Abortion Act is a reliable precedent, then I fear that we may create a situation in which the vulnerable are made more vulnerable. Compassion may be replaced by function.

Without claiming that the legalization of abortion and euthanasia are identical, the politics of the two do have a certain affinity. On the issue of abortion (and on divorce) in the 1960s the Church of England's Board of Social Responsibility supported changes in the law, but discovered later that the actual changes *de facto* were far more permissive than intended. In the 1960s there was widespread support in society at large and among churchgoers for a change in the law on compassionate grounds. The Bourne case, just before the war, had raised public consciousness in this area. By the early 1960s it was argued that there were strong compassionate reasons for changing the law—especially for women who had been raped, for under-age girls or those with learning disabilities too severe to be aware of the consequences of sexual intercourse, and for those whose health was severely at risk. It was also argued, using a mixture of compassionate and pragmatic grounds, that induced abortion was a fact of life and could be done safely by public (or private but legal) health services or at considerable risk to the women involved by illegal abortionists. The 1968 Abortion Law was widely seen as a compassionate response, allowing for abortion for the disadvantaged. Yet very quickly it was realized that a liberty for the few on compassionate grounds had become a right for women on any grounds. Abortion clinics soon argued that since early abortion was safer for the woman than having a baby, then abortion in the first trimester at least could always be justified in terms of the Abortion Law.

This, I believe, is still the central dilemma confronting attempts to legalize euthanasia in its strict sense. Given the way legal systems inevitably work, how can we prevent a liberty being turned effectively into a right? This is *de facto* what has happened in the Netherlands. The House of Lords' *Report on Medical Ethics* argued that strict grounds for euthanasia are simply not applied there. In addition, it has become increasingly difficult to get juries in the Netherlands to convict doctors who disregard official procedures. It seems that once a line is crossed on such issues, then any kind of control becomes ever more difficult.

My own fear is that by introducing legislation in this area on compassionate grounds we may create a society which is distinctly less compassionate. In such a society the elderly may feel pressured not to continue their lives at the expense of the young. The permanently disabled may feel the same. The health service may put less resources into palliative and geriatric care. In short, we will have become a less compassionate society—a society even more distant from the injunctions of Matthew 25.

In the absence of legislation we will, of course, still have problems. For example, there is continuing debate about what guidelines are appropriate for the permanently comatose—in terms both of the reliability of diagnoses and of the degree of consciousness of those deemed to be in a 'permanent vegetative state'. There are continuing moral debates about the status of withholding and especially withdrawing treatment and/or intensive nursing care. Nevertheless, experience from the legislation on abortion should, I believe, make Christians cautious about the possibility of legislation on euthanasia.

So my own position remains cautious despite the growing pressure from public opinion allied to the dilemmas raised by modern medicine. I fear that we are still too confused to legislate safely in this area.

Notes

1. See further Robin Gill, *Moral Leadership in a Postmodern Age* (Edinburgh: T. & T. Clark, 1997), chapter 10.
2. Peter Singer, *Rethinking Life and Death* (Oxford: Oxford University Press, 1995).
3. From *The City of God*, tr. Henry Bettenson, ed. David Knowles (Harmondsworth: Penguin, 1972), I.17.
4. The data used here were made available through Data Archive. The data were originally collected by the ESRC Research Centre on Microsocial Change at the University of Essex. Neither the original collectors of the data nor the Archive bear any responsibility for the analyses or interpretations presented here.
5. For a discussion, see Roger Jowell, John Curtice, Alison Park, Lindsay Brook and Katarina Thomson (eds), *British Social Attitudes: The 13th Report* (Dartmouth, NH: Social and Community Planning Research, 1996).
6. Committee on Medical Ethics, Episcopal Diocese of Washington DC, *Assisted Suicide and Euthanasia: Christian Moral Perspectives: The Washington Report* (Harrisburg, PA: Morehouse Publishing, 1997), p. 67.

Response by Peter Howdle

I am pleased to respond to this paper by Robin Gill. I write as a practising physician, a teacher of medical students and an active medical researcher. Questions raised by this topic impinge at a practical or theoretical level on all areas of my professional activity.

Professor Gill states the current position correctly. However, although the United States Supreme Court judgment does rule that physician-assisted suicide is not a fundamental right of the US Constitution, it is left to the individual States to rule whether or not to ban or legalize the practice. In using the term 'physician-assisted suicide' the US ruling is referring to a strict definition of euthanasia, one which Robin Gill uses as the basis for his thesis. Like him, I think this is a good starting point, since it is important to be clear what we are discussing. However, in everyday clinical practice, and in the minds of many lay people, it is not this working definition which prompts thought on the subject. There are indeed very few clear situations. We are more commonly in the realm of passive euthanasia, where the life of the terminally ill patient might or might not be shortened, and where 'quality of life' becomes all-important—Robin Gill's 'ambiguous situation'.

It may be helpful to comment specifically on Robin Gill's four areas of change.

First, changing attitudes in society towards euthanasia are clearly described, with some very useful data. I do not think that these data are particularly surprising: I would expect many people to support euthanasia for the terminally ill and fewer for those who are 'tired of living'. This phrase, and the reasons for such a state, raise enormous questions about identity, individuality, community and available resources and, as Robin Gill suggests, it is certainly not a question in relation to euthanasia which we can ignore.

Second, changes in medicine. There have certainly been great technological advances. However, we must keep things in perspective. We are not in a science-fiction age as often depicted by over-enthusiastic journalists or Hollywood. In the majority of patients where death seems inevitable, nature is allowed to take its course. In only a minority is technical life support possible or reasonable and even then its role is often very limited. The Tony Bland situation is the exception rather than the norm. This is not to argue that there are no questions to be addressed, simply that modern medicine has not fundamentally changed those questions.

Regarding changes in theology, where an amateur should be wary, my mind was excited by Robin Gill's exposition. I am not sure that referring to human life as a gift from God is very meaningful. Modern molecular genetics reveals much randomness and chance in our make-up, reflecting that shown in all creation by particle physics. As a Christian, I am deeply convinced of God being in the midst of all this, but I do not find the concept of giver and receiver helpful. Rather, for me as a Christian doctor, when I view human life from an eternal dimension, all things are seen to be in God's creative purposes. Death itself therefore does not signify finality and failure—but one has then to guard against viewing euthanasia as a utilitarian device.

Finally, changes in the law are mentioned. I think Robin Gill places too much emphasis on comparisons with the abortion legislation. There are many examples of well-drafted and administered law which is for the general good. I cannot see why euthanasia could not be properly legalized if that is what society wanted or thought permissible. The 'slippery slope' argument should not prevent us from taking careful steps where appropriate.

Robin Gill is concerned with society becoming less compassionate, and rightly so. Certainly, opinions about the need for euthanasia may be influenced by the way society fails to care properly for the disabled, the chronically sick, or those 'tired of life'. Conversely, some would argue that if the best facilities were available for the care of everyone in need then euthanasia in fact would not be an issue. I suspect, however, that both philosophically and practically it is not as easy as that,

Regarding my own position on the legalization of euthanasia, I would want to be more adventurous than Robin Gill would let us be. I could contemplate the possibility, and would want a continuing debate on the issue. It would help me in trying to discern the best way of providing healing for an individual patient.

Response by Ian Leck

This paper is a thoughtful and accessible appraisal of the case for euthanasia and the reasons why Christians are taking this case more seriously than they once did. All I want to criticize are Gill's definition of euthanasia and, more importantly, his failure to look explicitly at what a belief in life after death and the 'Love your neighbour as yourself' ethic imply about euthanasia.

As a definition of euthanasia, 'assistance or action intended to end the life of a human being *for her or his own sake*' seems more apt than Gill's '*medical* assistance or action which is intended to end a human life'. The latter definition would cover a doctor ending someone's life for any reason (e.g. financial gain if the doctor was expecting a legacy), and would exclude cases where a non-medical person tries to cut short the suffering of a dear friend or relative who is terminally ill. When discussing ethics, the motivation of the person who attempts to end another's life surely matters more than their profession.

This reference to motivation leads me to reflect on 'Love your neighbour as yourself'. If for Christians this is the one fundamental commandment on how people should relate to each other, so that 'he who loves his neighbour has met every requirement of the law' (Romans 13:8), should not the search for a Christian ethic about euthanasia start here? If you try to love your neighbour as yourself, may there not come a time when this will motivate you to end a neighbour's life, if she or he is suffering so much as to want to die, and if you would yourself want to die if you were suffering like this? Although Gill does not mention this line of thought, it is one that may well feed into the 'increasing challenge within churches and among theologians' that he sees confronting the Christian tradition of opposition to euthanasia.

This challenge may also be fuelled by changes in what Christians believe about life after death. The traditional teaching that death led to heaven for some but to hell for many more, and that one's destination might depend on how one faced death, may have offered more hope than the expectation of gloom for all in Hades or Sheol which this teaching replaced: but for many it probably heightened the fear of death and the desire to delay it for as long as possible. However, many of us now reject the idea of eternal hell-fire, since God's purpose is 'to show mercy to all mankind' (Romans 11:32). We believe that the worst that may happen after death is oblivion, and that dying can be viewed positively, as a time to 'give thee back the life I owe, that in thine ocean depths its flow may richer, fuller be' (*Hymns and Psalms* 685). Gill echoes this verse when he writes that 'when God-given life becomes nothing but a burden, it might seem appropriate to return that life . . . to the giver'; but he does not explore how ideas about life after death affect attitudes to euthanasia.

Thinking as I do about love and death, I believe that there are occasions when euthanasia is in principle ethical. I share Gill's anxiety that if we totally decriminalize it 'on compassionate grounds we may create a society which is . . . less compassionate', i.e., we may not be promoting the greatest good of the greatest number. However, I believe that the law is wrong to treat as murder, and prescribe life imprisonment for, the ending of a life by someone motivated by love and not malice.

Response by Julie Norris

Robin Gill's lecture plotted shifts in medicine, theology and public opinion regarding euthanasia. He showed that opposition to euthanasia has lessened, and that significant numbers of people now favour the legalization of voluntary euthanasia. Gill noted that public awareness of medical change has fostered this favourable attitude. People live longer, the incidence of severe degenerative illness increases and sometimes attempts to save life result in people living in a persistent vegetative state. But this is only part of the picture. Post-modern influences have also their part to play in the changing attitudes towards euthanasia. Under the influence of social critics (e.g. Gadamer) a plethora of new interpretations of context and tradition have burst into the public domain. Whereas previous generations were constrained by various kinds of authority, the post-modern state is open and there are many different voices to be heard. There is suspicion of claims to absolute truth, and there is a stress on the individual's freedom to make their own choices. This is reflected in the words of Bob Dent, 'If you disagree with voluntary euthanasia then don't use it. But don't deny me the right to use it.' He became the first person to die as a result of legal voluntary euthanasia, after the Northern Territory of Australia passed legislation in 1996 (a law which was later revoked). The growing emphasis on the freedom of the individual to choose what happens to their own body, and in particular to choose what happens at the end of their life, will eventually be the determining factor, I think, in pushing us towards legalizing euthanasia in this country whether we in the churches like it or not.

Some theologians have been influenced by the interpretative tools and methods of the post-modern theories. Their willingness to look in different ways at texts, tradition and context, has made it possible to consider fresh perspectives which would have been condemned out of hand in previous generations and this has broadened the ethical debate. Thus Gill charted the relaxation of the traditional condemnation of euthanasia for some Christians.

But this is only one side of the picture. The Roman Catholic Church is one of those which stands as a citadel against all pressures to change its traditional condemnation of euthanasia. In his encyclical *Veritatis Splendor*, the Pope rejected claims of personal autonomy and the belief that human beings can do what they want with their own bodies. In *Evangelium Vitae*, he utterly opposed euthanasia as one aspect of the 'culture of death' which threatens the sanctity of life and the fabric of society.

Gill helpfully showed that there were theological arguments for both the pro- and anti-euthanasia positions and that there was some common ground between the two. He did not, however, explain the irreconcilable theological differences between the alternative views, or the acute problems that euthanasia presents to some theologies. It is the question of the sanctity of life which lies at the heart of the Christian debate about euthanasia, and Gill did not do this argument justice. The Roman Catholic and pro-life positions suggest that, no matter what extenuating circumstances there are, human life is so sacred that it is inviolable. This is reflected in *Evangelium Vitae* in the discussion about abortion in which the Pope declares 'No circumstance, no purpose, no law whatsoever can ever make licit an act which is illicit'. Indeed taking the life of another person seems to step over a limit, and not just to cheapen life but also to threaten the cohesion of society by breaking one of the most basic moral prohibitions.

This position is irreconcilable with the pro-euthanasia view which makes distinctions between different kinds of life and wants to meet different situations with a variety of responses. It is not that life is valueless, but that some extreme situations call for compassionate interference to end suffering. Far from cheapening life, this acknowledges the reality of suffering (which we some-times inadvertently create) and becomes an act of responsibility. It also takes seriously the blurring of the edges of life, seen most clearly in cases of persistent vegetative state. John Habgood said 'How much of the human body needs to be dead before it can be said that the human being is dead?' Although Gill represented the arguments in favour of euthanasia, he did not recognize the strength of the principled opposition that there would be to any attempt to legalize euthanasia, from the pro-life and Roman Catholic stances.

Gill drew some parallels between euthanasia and abortion and argued that the introduction of the abortion law was the begin-ning of the move towards euthanasia. Although arguments from the sanctity of human life do lead to a rejection of both abortion and euthanasia, consideration of the two issues from the point of view of someone who does not consider all life to be the same requires that the issues be treated separately. An embryo may be valued for its future potential, whereas a terminally ill person belongs to a myriad of relationships—these two are quite distinct. There seems to be some justification in the argument that aligning abortion and euthanasia leads to confusion.

Gill's other reservations about legalizing euthanasia need serious consideration. They reflect some of the concerns expressed in the Select Committee of the House of Lords' Report in 1994. Gill was concerned that the practice of euthanasia would be difficult to control and that vulnerable people might be abused. He argued that legalizing euthanasia for compassionate reasons could ultimately create a less compassionate society. Some of his fears are reinforced by observations of voluntary euthanasia in the Netherlands where bad practice (some non-voluntary euthanasia) and general confusion has been reported. But perhaps such a situation is inevitable given the ambiguity of the legal situation there. It does not follow that in another country, with clearer and better enforced legislation, the same problems would arise. Indeed it might be possible to overcome Gill's reservations by careful legislation, good monitoring of practice, and proper accountability of those who carry out euthanasia.

If voluntary euthanasia were legalized in this country, I would like to see a body set up to authorize and monitor each case. Such a move would also minimize any detrimental effect that legalizing euthanasia might have on the doctor–patient relationship, since it would not be the doctor who made the decision.

Personally I think that it is only a matter of time before conditional voluntary euthanasia is introduced in this country. It will never receive universal approval but neither will it lead to the disintegration of our society.

Reply by Robin Gill

These are three courteous and thoughtful responses to my paper on euthanasia. The issue of euthanasia is likely to divide Christians and others for some time to come. It raises passions and emotions and sometimes those arguing about it can become quite abusive. Not so here. I am most grateful for that and for the care with which each of the respondents has read my paper.

Perhaps I can begin by expressing points of agreement. Peter Howdle is right to point to the July 1997 judgment of the US Supreme Court, which raises a very important issue to which I will return in a moment—namely, what is sometimes termed 'procedural deterioration'. This is the fear, expressed by the Supreme Court, that a change in law in this area, for the best of intentions, may gradually lead to an erosion of legal process. Peter Howdle's point about keeping medical changes in perspective is also helpful. PVS (persistent vegetative state), as in the Tony Bland case for example, remains important for ethics because it is so intractable, although from a clinical perspective it is relatively rare. One estimate suggests that in Britain there may be about a thousand PVS cases at the moment. I also agree with his theological point that death 'does not signify finality and failure' and that 'all things are seen to be in God's creative purposes'.

Ian Leck helpfully points to the implications for euthanasia of different concepts of life after death. I share his disbelief in 'eternal hellfire', but can see that such a belief might change the debate. He may also be right that 'the law is wrong to treat as murder the ending of a life by someone motivated by love and not malice'. There is a good case to be made that the mandatory life sentence confronting any doctor found guilty of euthanasia is wrong. Doctors who act in good faith and not for personal gain should not be tried as if they are simply murderers. Even at a pragmatic level, the mandatory life sentence here may be counter-productive: juries have consistently shown that they are most unwilling to find any doctor guilty when a life sentence is the only punishment allowed by law.

Julie Norris argues that I did not explain 'the irreconcilable theological differences between the alternative views or the acute problems that euthanasia presents to some theologies'. She cites the very strong position taken in *Evangelium Vitae*. She may well be right about this. However, since I have recently published responses to *Evangelium Vitae* and *Veritatis Splendor*, I was not keen to go over the same ground again here. My purpose was more limited: it was simply to show how a theological concept such as God-givenness has been used in both sides of the euthanasia debate.

On all of this we agree. Our main disagreement is about the possible effects of legislation. Would a cautious attempt to legalize euthanasia lead to a less caring medical environment? I believe that it would, but at least two of the respondents believe that it would not.

Our disagreement here is about procedural deterioration. It was precisely to demonstrate this that I gave the extended illustration of legalizing abortion. Obviously abortion and euthanasia are different ethical issues, as Julie Norris and Peter Howdle both emphasize. However, the legal procedure surrounding them may be similar. Changing public attitudes arising from widespread compassion for those suffering in a crisis situation (e.g. women who are raped or those dying painfully from incurable illnesses) act as the spur for legalization. At this stage it is emphasized that legalization is for those in crisis and involves careful and judicious selection. People must have very serious grounds for having abortions/euthanasia and they certainly should not feel pressurized by their families. However, once legalized a morally pluralistic society finds judicious selection difficult to enforce. A liberty for the few becomes a licence for the many. In addition, those seeking abortion/euthanasia soon demand it as a 'right'. Thus, without ever having legalized pro-choice abortion, in reality that is what we now have in Britain. Furthermore, the public has now come to accept this. In a recent MORI poll four-fifths of those interviewed agreed with abortion on pro-choice grounds.

This is what is meant by procedural deterioration. Whatever our personal view, we now have abortion on demand in Britain, and all of the safeguards built into the Abortion Act have been bypassed. My fear is that this is exactly what will happen with euthanasia. Julie Norris's idea about 'a body set up to authorize and monitor each case' simply does not answer this problem. It would soon be challenged in law by determined individuals and undermined by

our moral pluralism. Nor will Ian Leck's attempt to limit euthanasia to the ending of the life of a human being 'for her or his own
sake', since it ignores those cases where the demand for active
euthanasia is strongest but the wishes of the patient are unknow-
able (e.g. for people like Tony Bland).

I deliberately avoided the term 'slippery slope' in my paper and
wrote instead about 'crossing a line'. My fear remains that if we
cross this particular line, we will make the vulnerable more vulnerable. For the best of motives we will actually make things worse.
I still fear that we are too morally confused to legislate safely in this
area. Nonetheless I am most grateful for these three thoughtful
responses.

Section 2

Should Christians accept the validity of voluntary euthanasia?

PAUL BADHAM

What sort of euthanasia is being considered?

The kind of voluntary euthanasia I wish to discuss is when a person in the final stages of a terminal illness requests medical assistance in terminating his or her own life. I am thinking of a legal framework like that of the Netherlands, where no legal or professional hazard applies to a doctor who accedes to such a request under a number of given conditions. The first condition must be that there is clear and convincing evidence of enduring free determination by the patient so that there is no doubt at all of the patient's wish for his or her life to be ended. Second, the patient's decision must be an informed one, made after full discussion with the doctors and in awareness of all relevant facts. Third, the patient must face irreversible, protracted and unbearable suffering. And finally there must be, from the patient's viewpoint, an absence of reasonable alternatives to alleviate the suffering.[1] When euthanasia is practised in such conditions, no doctor in the Netherlands will be successfully prosecuted.

The purpose of this paper is to argue that were such a framework of law to be established in Britain, it would be entirely appropriate for a believing and practising Christian patient to request the termination of his or her life, and equally appropriate for a believing and practising Christian doctor to accede to such a request.

Would the expansion of palliative care remove the need for euthanasia?

It is frequently claimed that modern advances in palliative care have so improved the care of the dying that instances of ir-reversible, protracted and unbearable suffering ought to be extremely rare. Hence the case for permitting euthanasia is no longer as strong as it was. I rejoice in such developments, and very much hope that the spread of palliative medicine and hospice care will enable more people to die in dignity and peace without the need to resort to euthanasia. But this does not weaken the case for allowing euthanasia in those cases where suffering remains inescapably present. There may also be patients for whom the prospect of permanent and continuous sedation under morphine or heroin is not an acceptable alternative to suffering, and who would continue to prefer that their life be brought to an end. It would seem right that this choice should be available to them.

In practice it remains the case that many people continue to suffer greatly during their terminal illness. The distinguished Yale physician Sherwin Nuland, in his recent work *How We Die*, documents just how devastating the process of dying usually is. Nuland believes that we do people a grave disservice if we lead them to believe that they can expect to die with dignity, or that their suffering can always be alleviated. He believes that the trauma of dying for both patient and family has been greatly intensified in recent years because people have been misled into believing that modern medication can control the suffering. Nuland believes the odds are overwhelmingly against this.[2] I am not in a position to adjudicate between Nuland and those he criticizes. I can only say that what Nuland says seems to have been true for every death I have personally witnessed and that the perusal of the death columns in any daily newspaper shows that 'after much suffering, bravely borne' continues to be a common prelude to our last hours.

Must voluntary euthanasia lead to involuntary euthanasia?

It is often argued that any legalization on voluntary euthanasia will lead to an acceptance of involuntary euthanasia and indeed that this has already happened in the Netherlands. The Submission from the Ethics Group of the Association for Palliative Medicine to the House of Lords' Committee on Medical Ethics showed that in the Netherlands 1.8 per cent of deaths are now due to voluntary euthanasia and 0.8 per cent to involuntary euthanasia.[3] This statistic on its own might be slightly misleading, for the report makes clear that in nearly all such cases the decision was made in consultation with nurses and the family in circumstances where the patient was near death and in unbearable pain. In over 50 per cent of the cases the decision was also taken in the knowledge that the patient had expressed in advance a wish for euthanasia if such circumstances were ever reached.[4] It seems likely therefore that at least in the vast majority of cases involuntary euthanasia was given under circumstances where both family and doctors took the decision on behalf of the patient believing that this would have been their choice if they had been in a position to articulate it. It does not seem clear that for the family to act on behalf of the patient in this way, particularly in the light of the patient's known wishes, is necessarily an illegitimate extension of the principle of voluntary euthanasia.

But there are obvious dangers in such a development. One is that the existence of a legal framework which tolerates euthanasia evokes a state of fear in at least some old people. There is anecdotal evidence that some elderly people in the Netherlands are consciously choosing nursing homes in Germany to avoid a perceived risk of being 'put down' against their will. This is not an insuperable problem since if euthanasia were legally permitted in Britain, hospices could be forbidden to practise it. This might well solve the problem and should cause no additional difficulties, first because the directors of hospices are known to oppose any change in the law, second because they have the greatest access to palliative care which in most cases alleviates any need for euthanasia. Third, patients who choose hospices do so because they want the security and care of what these offer.

However, the argument concerning fear works both ways. I accept that allowing euthanasia at all will make some elderly people feel fearful. But there is abundant evidence that the lack of a euthanasia law provokes other kinds of fears in elderly people, namely the fear they will be forced to suffer the agony of a long-drawn-out battle against death which doctors will fight over the battlefield of their bodies, in defiance of their wishes. Nuland's book *How We Die* provides detailed evidence of how well justified this fear is. And Nowell Smith, sometime President of the international Federation of Right to Die Societies, shows what a high proportion of the population share this fear.[5]

On balance, patients may have more to fear from the treatment they are likely to receive in the absence of a euthanasia law than from the risk of involuntary euthanasia in the presence of such a law. There is always a danger of sliding down slippery slopes. But the danger of the slippery slope does not in itself prevent one from arguing that unambiguously voluntary euthanasia ought to be allowed. Moreover, as we shall see later, new data from the Netherlands suggest that the notion that permitting euthanasia involves such a slide may not be justified by the realities of the Dutch experience.

Can a Bible-believing Christian legitimately choose death for him- or herself?

To many this will seem a strange question, because it is widely believed that 'The Everlasting has . . . fixed his canon gainst self-slaughter!' Hence, the 'calamity of so long a life' must be endured and we must be reconciled to 'rather bear those ills we have, than fly to others that we know not of'.[6] But this is Shakespeare, speaking through Hamlet. It is not the case that the canonical scriptures forbid suicide. They forbid murder, and hence perhaps by implication suicide, but the implication is not spelt out and suicides are recorded in the Bible without condemnation. Let me quickly illustrate this by running through the suicides recorded in the Bible.

Samson is said to have been given strength by God to pull the house of Dagon down upon his own head so that he would die with his enemies.[7] The suicides of King Saul and of his armour-bearer in order to escape the humiliation of capture and mockery are reported without any negative comment and their deaths were lamented by the whole of Israel.[8] Eleazar Avaran is said to have 'given his life to save his people and to win himself an everlasting name' by stabbing a war elephant from beneath so it fell on him and killed him as well as the enemies whom it carried.[9] Razis 'fell upon his own sword, preferring to die nobly than to fall into the hands of sinners and suffer outrages unworthy of his noble birth'.[10] In none of these cases is there any hint of disapproval. In the New Testament we are of course told that Judas Iscariot hanged himself, but this is simply reported without comment.[11] The woe predicated on Judas was prior to the suicide, not consequential upon it.[12]

For Christians the foundation for ethical behaviour is the imitation of Christ. Historically he died a cruel death at the hands of his enemies. Yet strangely the fourth Gospel presents it as the product of Jesus' own choice to lay down his life: 'No one takes it from me, I lay it down of my own accord.'[13] In one of Jesus' best loved parabolic images he pictures himself as a good shepherd ready to lay down his life for his sheep, and what is often overlooked is that the imagery makes no sense except on the supposition that a caring shepherd would indeed normally make such a choice.[14] Jesus also taught that a readiness to die for another is the ultimate true test of friendship, 'Greater love has no man than this that a man lay down his life for his friends'.[15] Such sayings are not directly relevant to euthanasia, though it is interesting to recall that these verses came into the mind of Scott in the Antarctic when the dying Captain Oates walked out into the snow to perish quickly and thereby enhance the chances of survival for all his colleagues. But what such verses do legitimately teach is that death is not the ultimate evil to be avoided at all costs. It is something which can be legitimately embraced as a positive good. The sanctity of life is not a biblical absolute. It is a value which has to be balanced against other values.

The Christian acceptance of death

Acceptance of death in a positive spirit was for centuries perceived as a normative Christian attitude. St Paul seems consciously to have chosen to go to Jerusalem even though he knew that such a decision would probably lead to his death.[16] Yet he felt no concern about this prospect: 'I am on the point of being sacrificed; the time of my departure has come. I have fought a good fight. I have finished my course. I have kept the faith. Henceforth there is laid up for me a crown of righteousness.'[17] During centuries of persecution, a willingness to die for faith was deemed to be one of the supreme Christian virtues, and in the last century missionaries willingly went out to 'the white man's grave' of malarial West Africa for the sake of the Christian Gospel.

It is true of course that acts of great bravery in battle, or willingness to face martyrdom or high risk of disease for the sake of spreading the Gospel, are not what is meant by suicide. In practice, death may have been virtually certain, but it was not chosen. It was simply the by-product of another choice, namely to use all possible means to defeat an enemy, or to remain totally faithful even unto death. On the other hand such choices do draw attention to the fact that the Christian tradition does not see death as a fate to be avoided at all costs, but may in effect be legitimately accepted for some sufficient cause.

The question that has to be addressed is whether a swift death of one's own choosing can be legitimate for a Christian when the alternative is an agonizing, long-drawn-out, and ultimately futile battle with a terminal illness. From a biblical perspective the most relevant texts here would seem those which discuss the relative value of life in the context of terminal illness. Clearly there are abundant verses which speak of the value and worthwhileness of life when one is enjoying health and vigour. In such circumstances the thought of death is very bitter.[18] But when death comes at the end of a long life the situation is very different, 'O death how welcome is your sentence to one who is in need and is failing in strength, very old and distracted over everything; to one who is contrary, and has lost his patience!'[19] When a person loses his rationality the Bible says he would be better off dead for 'the life of the fool is worse than death'.[20] Likewise, faced with terminal illness, there is little point in clinging to life, for 'death is better than a miserable life, and eternal rest than chronic sickness'.[21] My argument is that it is precisely this judgement that a modern Christian should be allowed to make and to act upon in the closing stages of life.

A good case can be made for saying that from a biblical perspective and also from the perspective of the mainstream Christian tradition death is not something to be feared, but when it comes in the fullness of time it is to be welcomed. For example, in verse 6 of his famous 'Canticle of the Sun' Francis of Assisi included 'Sister Death' among the family of blessings for which we should sing God's praises. It is tragic that this dimension is so missing in contemporary Church life that modern hymn books asterisk this verse for suggested omission whenever the rest of the hymn is sung. Clearly editors today think that modern congregations would jib at praising 'most kind and gentle death' or of welcoming her as leading home the children of God.[22] Yet how much of the anguish currently associated with the futile and painful efforts of medical science to hold back the inevitable would be avoided if only attitudes like those of St Francis were once again common.

From a Christian perspective death is believed to be the gateway to a new, richer and fuller life with God. If such beliefs are true then when death comes in the fullness of time it should be embraced and accepted.

Does choosing death imply despairing of God's goodness?

We have already seen that the prohibition of suicide is not derived in any straightforward way from biblical teaching. It is, however, strongly associated with traditional assumptions about divine providence, the virtues of patience and suffering, and the sense that actually to kill oneself is ultimately to despair of the loving purposes of God. The presumption here is that an authentic Christian attitude shows itself in accepting in patience what God has willed. The problem is that the framework of belief here pre-supposed is not one which the typical contemporary Christian, whether priest or lay, seriously believes today.

The centre of the discussion hinges on how divine providence is understood as operating. In former ages most Christians believed that all aspects of life were under the direct and immediate control of God. On this view God was the immediate cause of all that happened, and the appropriate action for a Christian was to submit to what God had ordained. Hence illness was perceived as being either a judgement on sin or a trial of patience, and the time of a person's death was seen as entirely a matter of divine decree. In accordance with such views Christians for many centuries forbade the giving of medicine,[23] the practice of surgery, the study of anatomy or the dissection of corpses for medical research. Later, the practices of inoculation and vaccination faced fierce theological opposition, as did the initial use of quinine against malaria.[24] The introduction of anaesthesia and, above all, the use of chloroform in childbirth were seen as directly challenging the divine edict that 'in pain you shall bring forth children',[25] and hence were violently denounced from public pulpits throughout Britain and the United States.[26]

The root objection to all the medical practices mentioned above was the belief that the duty of human beings was to submit in patience to what God had willed. All innovations in medical prac- tice were initially seen as implying a lack of faith and trust in God's good purposes. Doctors were accused of 'playing God', of being unwilling to accept that God knows what is right for a particular

person, of prying into sacred mysteries and areas of God's own pre-
rogative.[27] Yet, gradually, all mainstream Christian Churches have
modified their teaching and the formerly criticized activity of the
doctor has come to be seen as itself a channel of God's love and the
vehicle of his providence. Consequently, although the practice of
medicine faced opposition in earlier centuries, a very close relationship now often exists between doctors and clergy, and medically
trained missionaries have made a substantial contribution to the
worldwide diffusion of Western medicine. Christians today are
happy to think of doctors as fulfilling the will of God in restoring
to health persons struck down by curable illness. What I wish to
suggest is that a doctor might equally be seen as an agent of
divine providence in bringing a life to a peaceful end where no
realistic hope of recovery exists.

One of the oldest Christian hymns is a prayer to God for a good
death: 'grant to life's day a calm unclouded ending, / an eve
untouched by shadows of decay'.[28] If this is something we can
legitimately ask God to grant it would be odd to suppose that we
cannot make a comparable request to those whom we recognize as
continuing God's gracious work.

Is it good for us to suffer?

One traditional Christian objection to euthanasia is that suffering
is part of life, given by God to school our character and test our for-
titude. To opt out of suffering is a repudiation of the opportunities
that suffering provides for spiritual growth. What a dying
Christian should do is rather to unite his or her sufferings with the
sufferings of Christ and to offer them up to God. Taking this view,
the pain and deprivation of terminal illness is something to be
stoically accepted as part of the total experience of life, which must
be endured and not run away from. The argument is open to two
serious objections. The first is that the theory does not correspond
with human experience, since there is a great deal of evidence to
show that suffering however bravely borne is rarely ennobling. The
second is that the theory ought not to be used as an argument

against euthanasia unless one were prepared to accept other implications of the hypothesis and refrain from administering analgesics. Yet virtually no one today takes that line. Almost everyone concerned with the dying accepts the duty and responsibility to do everything in one's power to minimize the discomfort of the terminally ill. The goal of palliative medicine is to search for a balance of medication at precisely the right dosage to control all pain. If suffering were genuinely believed to be good this is not the policy that would be followed.

However, given that alleviating pain is recognized as desirable, a further question arises consequential to this. If our experiences in this life are seen theologically as a means of growth and development, it is hard to see that keeping life going under constant medication helps in a Christian understanding of what life is for. Many who value above all their sentience and rationality would rather endure pain than spend their final days in a dream-world of narcotic illusion. Such people might well wish to have their life ended while they were still in control of their faculties, rather than to continue for a few months longer as helpless dependants on heroin or morphine. This may be particularly true of those most committed to Christian values, who may well have fought against a drug culture throughout their lives and have no wish to succumb to it in their last weeks.

The implication of Christ's 'golden rule'

One key principle for a Christian ethic is the yardstick recommended by Jesus in what Christians regard as his 'golden rule' from the Sermon on the Mount, namely 'Always treat others as you would like them to treat you'.[29] Throughout life the hope is that if someone falls ill, he or she will be able to obtain medical help to be restored to life and vitality. On this principle one would seek to ensure that medical treatment was as widely available as possible to all persons suffering any kind of disease or infirmity whether of mind or body. Doctors and nurses who minister to the sick in this way are widely recognized by Christians as genuine agents and embodiments of God's providential love. Christians often describe the professions of medicine and nursing as 'vocations', that is, jobs to which people may feel called by God to undertake for the good of humanity. I suggest the same principle should be upheld when following the golden rule leads a doctor to help a patient out of terminal and hopeless misery. The suicide rate is far higher among doctors than among the general public because they have the knowledge and means to bring their own suffering to an end when they know their position is hopeless. The application of the golden rule suggests that it would be right if they were allowed to extend to others the same treatment that they are able to extend to themselves.

Is a request for euthanasia a denial of Christian hope?

Some suggest that to accept that one is not going to recover and therefore to request help to die is an act of faithless despair, a proclamation of hopelessness, and as such an offence against two of the central theological virtues—faith and hope. Here it is important that we confine ourselves to the very limited context of our discussion. We are considering cases where there are no realistic grounds for supposing that recovery is possible, and where even if some limited remission might occur, it would at best be temporary. There seems no virtue, whether theological or other, in self-delusion. Honest appraisal and a willingness to face reality seem far more appropriate stances. Moreover, it would be a total denial of the most basic Christian beliefs to limit hope to this world. As St Paul puts it, 'If it is for this life only that Christ has given us hope, we of all people are most to be pitied'.[30] And if we are speaking of hope in the context of the three theological virtues of faith, hope and love, it is worth reminding ourselves that from a New Testament perspective faith and love 'both spring from that hope stored up for you in heaven'.[31] When we speak of 'the Christian hope' we are speaking of the historic Christian belief in a life after death. This is the context in which faith and hope are being considered. In a situation where a person's life is clearly drawing to its close, it could be an affirmation of faith, hope and love for a person to voluntarily choose death, entrusting his or her destiny into the loving hands of God.

The understanding of God presupposed here is that picture of God which is most distinctive of Jesus, namely that God is like a loving Father always ready to accept his prodigal children.[32] Clearly, on some other understandings of God, suicide would be the ultimate folly. If God were like a heavenly tyrant who would damn a suicide to endless punishment on the analogy of a ruler who might sentence to death a deserter in time of war, then euthanasia would be an act of unimaginable folly. But this view of God is really incompatible with the picture given to us in the teaching of Jesus, and though accepted by some in the past has little support in contemporary Christianity. New Testament criticism has shown fairly conclusively that the analogy of fatherhood was very rare in ancient Judaism prior to Jesus, and yet was Jesus' own constant usage concerning God. It is also apparent that Jesus' teaching of the necessity for forgiveness was the most controversial aspect of his thought, and is therefore almost certainly distinctive of him. Given this, a Christian may feel confident that God would show the same love and care to an actual suicide as Jesus' contemporary followers in the Samaritan movement seek to show to those who only make the attempt.

A further consideration is that the image of a suicide as a deserter abandoning his post without permission is most inept in the case of euthanasia we are discussing. Given belief in any kind of providential order, one might conclude that the onslaught of terminal illness was the clearest indication of a divine intention to recall one to another station that could be given, and the person opting for euthanasia is merely making greater haste to respond to the divine summons. As David Hume put it in his classic essay 'whenever pain and sorrow so far overcome my patience, as to make me tired of life, I may conclude that I am recalled from my station in the clearest and most express terms'.[33] In the Bible the prophet Job reached the same conclusion, and in speech after speech describes the symptoms of his various illnesses as the harbingers of the death he longs for. 'Death would be better than these sufferings of mine. I have no desire to live.'[34]

Euthanasia as a letting-go of life

One important argument for euthanasia is that it is a natural extension of the success of modern medicine. It is precisely because modern medicine has made it possible for us to choose to resist death that it should also be allowed to help us to choose when to abandon that resistance. Much of what I advocate would be gained by a greater spirit of 'letting go' when there is no realistic hope of recovery. But this is not true of all cases. On some occasions when it becomes apparent that further resistance to the illness is futile, the medical measures previously taken to combat the disease will ensure that the process of dying will be prolonged and painful. Having already massively intervened in the natural process, it seems wrong to then make an arbitrary distinction between killing and letting-die to prevent the patient being given the help needed.

Can euthanasia be reconciled with our duty to protect the vulnerable?

One argument against the view set forth here is that any legislation to permit euthanasia on request would put psychological pressure on aged and infirm people to ask for it even though it was not their real wish. A Christian should support the view that the law should protect vulnerable and dependent members of society from being exposed to such pressure when they are at their most vulnerable. I accept that this argument draws attention to a real problem. No matter how carefully legislation is framed it could be abused in the way feared. But what this objection fails to take note of is that this pressure would work in both directions. If euthanasia were legalized, many aged people who actually wanted to die would be put under enormous psychological pressure from relatives and friends not to ask for euthanasia but to patiently endure their sufferings. At present of course the position is even worse for those of the terminally ill who want euthanasia. They are not merely under pressure not to choose it. They simply have no choice.

The problem of procedural deterioration

One of the main reasons why many oppose legislation to allow euthanasia in cases of unbearable pain in terminal illness is the problem of 'procedural deterioration'. What this refers to is the fact that permissive legislation tends to change the climate of thought and behaviour in such a way as to lead to consequences very different from those originally intended. Christians opposed to legislation permitting euthanasia are particularly sensitive in this regard. They know that in the 1960s the Church of England Board for Social Responsibility and comparable Non-conformist groups had issued a succession of reports 'arguing for changes in the *laws* relating to homosexual practice, abortion and divorce which closely foreshadowed the legislation subsequently passed'.[35] They also know that the impact of these laws was very different from what had been foreshadowed when the changes were urged. Those Church bodies who gave testimony to the Wolfenden Committee on homosexuality thought solely in terms of behaviour between 'consenting adults in private'. They never envisaged the possibility of the public 'outing' of homosexuality, or of television drama in which it might be presented as commonplace. The authors of the Anglican Report *Putting Asunder* of 1966[36] did not foresee the explosion in divorce which subsequently followed the Divorce Reform Act of 1969. Most significantly of all, Christian support for Abortion Law reform, typified by the Board of Social Responsibility report *Abortion: an Ethical Discussion*,[37] thought solely in terms of 'hard cases'. Christians could see a justification for abortion when the mother's life was in serious peril, or when there was a real risk of gross abnormality in the foetus. What was never foreseen was that legislation to allow abortion in such cases would lead to 170,000 legal abortions a year. Moreover, a briefing paper

'Abortion and the Church of England' sent to the Diocesan Bishops on 14 April 1997 shows that since the 1967 Abortion Act only 0.004 per cent of abortions have actually been carried out to save the life of the mother, and only 1.5 per cent have been performed to prevent 'serious foetal handicap'.[38]

The fear that a similar kind of procedural deterioration might apply in the case of euthanasia is undoubtedly the strongest argument against legislating for it. But is this fear justified? In what ways might permissive legislation to allow euthanasia parallel these earlier instances? It is already known that a majority of doctors admit that in some cases they have combated unbearable pain by increasing the dosage of morphine to a level which would have the 'unintended but foreseen' side-effect of shortening the patient's life. If euthanasia were to be legalized it would seem likely that some of these cases would be openly acknowledged as instances of euthanasia. To that extent there could be a parallel with the way permissive legislation encouraged society to be more acceptive of the existence of homosexuality, and more openly acknowledge that some marriages do 'irretrievably break down'. These parallels do not seem to raise moral issues for euthanasia.

Abortion is clearly perceived as the most problematic analogy. But in what does the supposed parallel consist? As Margaret Otlowski points out, the free availability of abortion

most certainly cannot be taken as evidence of a likely slide from voluntary to non-voluntary or involuntary euthanasia if the practice were to be legalized. Such a claim could only be made if there were evidence that the liberalization of abortion law so as to allow the practice in certain circumstances at a woman's request had led to abortions being performed on women without their consent. This is simply not the case, so the 'abortion analogy' does not hold up to scrutiny as a serious objection to the legalisation of active voluntary euthanasia.[39]

Against this, however, we must urge that in the British context the real parallel came at the earlier stage; namely that legislating for abortion in 'hard cases' led to abortion 'at a woman's request' and this had not been intended by the legislators. In the euthanasia instance the fear is that legislation intended to relate to cases of unbearable pain in terminal illness might lead to 'euthanasia on demand'. Whether this fear is justified or not can be ascertained by looking at the situation in the Netherlands where euthanasia has been permitted for over twenty years. There is a problem in doing such an evaluation in that until recently reliable scholarly information has been hard to get hold of. In the absence of such data opponents of euthanasia have cited 'atrocity stories' about the situation in the Netherlands which Dutch medical authorities strongly refute. According to the Royal Dutch Medical Association and the Dutch Society for Health Law, opponents of euthanasia have conveyed a 'very inaccurate and unreliable impression . . . about the extent and nature of the practice of voluntary euthanasia in that country'. To counter this the Dutch established a commission under the Chairmanship of Professor Remmelink, the Procurator-General of their Supreme Court, to find out how active voluntary euthanasia was actually working. The data provided by the Remmelink report show that 'voluntary euthanasia is in fact performed much less frequently than had earlier been thought'. Indeed, some commentators suggest that the figures show that 'there is no indication that active euthanasia on request is practised more often in the Netherlands than elsewhere'.[40] The difference is that in the Netherlands the fact that a doctor who follows the recognized guidelines will not be prosecuted means that the whole issue of the appropriate treatment of a terminally ill patient can be discussed with the patient. This means that instead of the doctor determining in isolation whether or not to increase the dosage of pain-killing drugs which the doctor knows will have the side-effect of bringing death forward, the doctor can now find out the patient's views about the matter. Ironically this means that far from leading doctors to slide down a slippery slope, the fact that euthanasia is always a possibility means that medical intervention to actively bring about death may become less needed. Thus, according to Helga Kuhse and Peter Singer 'the open practice of voluntary euthanasia may have reduced the incidence of doctors acting without the consent of the patient in ways that the doctor foresees will result in the patient's death'.[41]

The primacy of free choice

One much-used argument for euthanasia is the importance of individual freedom and autonomy to live and die in the ways that are most conducive to our well-being as persons. This appears to have been one of the benefits experienced by many in the Netherlands. The Remmelink figures show that 'a large number of patients seek assurance from their doctors that active voluntary euthanasia will be available if their suffering becomes intolerable'.[42] But only a few of these patients ever take advantage of this. Just to know the right exists brings them a sense of assurance and a peace of mind which enables them to cope better with their illness. They change from being simply victims of circumstance to persons who know they have some control over their destiny if their worst fears about the course of their illness come to be realized. What they value is living in a society where they are free to be, as far as possible, responsible for their own lives, and free to make their own decisions as to what treatment or help they wish to have. In an ideal society this should include the right to choose between adequate hospice care in the terminal stages of illness, or the equal right to seek for medical help to help them move on to what Christians hope will be the fuller life of the world to come.

The opportunity euthanasia offers for a prayerful death

Historically, it used to be the practice of all believers to summon a priest when death was thought near so that the patient could die surrounded by an atmosphere of prayer and worship, and in the presence of family and friends. Modern technology has largely taken away that option. Most of us will die alone in a hospital bed so wired up to saline drips and other support systems that the older death-bed scene ceases to be possible, and the dying process is so prolonged and extended as to cause weeks of strain and agony on all concerned. Yet if people were allowed and assisted to face the reality of the inevitable, it would be possible for death to become an affirmation. We can imagine a situation where a Christian could say goodbye to family and friends, a Holy Communion service could be celebrated at the believer's bedside, and he or she could be given the last rites in preparation for the journey through death to the life immortal. In a context of faith this would seem a far more Christian way of death than the present lonely and degrading extension of the dying process.

[*A shorter version of this paper appeared in* Studies in Christian Ethics, **8***(2), 1995, 1–12 and this expanded version is reprinted with their permission.*]

Notes

1. Marvin Newman, 'Voluntary active euthanasia' in Paul Badham et al., *Perspectives on Death and Dying* (Philadelphia: The Charles Press, 1989), p. 179.
2. Sherwin Nuland, *How We Die* (London: Chatto & Windus, 1994), p. 263.
3. *Submission from the Ethics Group of the Association for Palliative Medicine of Great Britain and Ireland* to the Select Committee of the House of Lords on Medical Ethics, 1993, p. 25.
4. Ibid., p. 17.
5. P. Nowell Smith, 'The right to die' in Paul Badham, *Ethics on the Frontiers of Human Existence* (New York: Paragon House, 1992).
6. W. Shakespeare, *Hamlet*, Act I, Sc. 2, lines 129ff.; Act III, Sc. 1, lines 56ff.
7. Judges 17:28–30.
8. 1 Samuel 31:3–6; 2 Samuel 1:11–27.
9. 1 Maccabees 6:44.
10. 2 Maccabees 14:41–42.
11. Matthew 27:5.
12. Matthew 26:24.
13. John 10:18.
14. John 10:10–16.
15. John 15:13.
16. Acts 20:16–38.
17. 1 Timothy 4:6–8.
18. Sirach 41:1.
19. Sirach 41:2.

20. Sirach 22:11.
21. Sirach 30:17.
22. In the translation published in *Hymns Ancient and Modern Revised* (London: William Clowes, 1950), hymn 172, verse 6.
23. The giving of medicine is explicitly forbidden in the early Christian book of teaching called the *Didache* 2:2. It may also be forbidden in the Bible in Galatians 5:20 where *pharmakeia* is banned. Although often now translated as a ban on sorcery, reference to any Greek dictionary will make clear that its primary meaning is 'medicine' or 'drug', and this is the meaning of 'pharmacy' in almost all other contexts.
24. Cf. A. D. White, *A History of the Warfare of Science with Theology in Christendom* (Cambridge, MA: Harvard University Press, 1955), vol. 2, pp. 33ff.
25. Genesis 3:16.
26. A. D. White, *Warfare of Science with Theology*, vol. 2, p. 63.
27. Ibid., ch. 13.
28. From 'O Strength and Stay Upholding All Creation'.
29. Matthew 7:12.
30. 1 Corinthians 15:19.
31. Colossians 1:5.
32. Luke 15:11–32.
33. David Hume, 'On suicide' in R. Wollheim, *Hume on Religion* (London: Fontana, 1963), p. 259.
34. Job 7:15; cf. 3:20–21, 7:3–7, 9:21, 10:1.
35. Christie Davies, 'Religion, politics and the permissive legislation' in Paul Badham, *Religion, State and Society in Modern Britain* (Lampeter: Mellen, 1989), p. 321.
36. Church of England Board for Social Responsibility, *Putting Asunder* (London: SPCK, 1966).
37. Church of England Board for Social Responsibility, *Abortion: An Ethical Discussion* (London: Church Information Office, 1965).
38. Editorial in *Theology*, C(796), July/Aug. 1997, p. 241.
39. Margaret Otlowski, *Voluntary Euthanasia and the Common Law* (Oxford: Clarendon, 1997), p. 223.
40. Ibid., p. 437.
41. H. Kuhse and P. Singer, editorial in *Bioethics*, 3, 1992, p. 4, cited in Margaret Otlowski, *Voluntary Euthanasia and the Common Law*, p. 439.
42. Margaret Otlowski, *Voluntary Euthanasia and the Common Law*, p. 441.

Response by Helen Oppenheimer

Paul Badham argues that if euthanasia became legal, within a framework like that of the Netherlands, it would be 'appropriate' for a Christian patient to ask for it and for a Christian doctor to co-operate. His primary question is the ethics of suicide. A change in the law is a prerequisite for his argument, because otherwise the objection would stand that to break the law is wrong in itself for patients and for doctors.

He does not always untangle the questions 'Should the law be changed?' and 'If it were, should euthanasia be acceptable to Christians?' The word 'appropriate' fails to unravel the distinctions between 'What ought a Christian individual to do?', 'What conduct should Christians refrain from condemning?' and 'What can Christians require of others, morally or legally?' If the differences between the desirable and the permissible are blurred, we are brought a little closer to the top of the slippery slope which leads gently from the right to end one's life to the duty to end one's life, and so to the right or even duty to end the life of someone we believe would be better dead.

Paul Badham is well aware of the slippery slope, but his caution does not prevail against his missionary spirit about voluntary euthanasia as a truly merciful release. His arguments are humane and telling, and it may seem legalistic or even bigoted to reject them. Let me say at once that I am not inclined to base the case against euthanasia on the Bible. The sanctity of life, I agree, 'is not a biblical absolute'. A Christian can hardly suppose that death is the 'ultimate evil'. But should we be so carried away as to embrace it as a positive good?

His examples do not prove his case. Jesus did not want to die, as the Gospels make very clear, but chose to lay down his life for our salvation. The martyrs who followed his example endured what their enemies did to them, even to the death. Captain Oates who walked out into the snow, hastening his death for the sake of his friends, was no suicide. Samson heroically pulled down the house of Dagon in order to kill the Philistines, not in order to kill himself.

These examples make the essential point, which indeed Paul Badham goes on to make. He even emphasizes it, ignoring the damage it does to his argument. Death, accepted though not chosen, may be 'the by-product of another choice'. In other words, the principle of double effect is no casuistical trick but a proper use of casuistry to analyse what is really happening. It has recently been made clear that a doctor may give potentially lethal painkillers to a patient dying of motor neurone disease, without risking prosecution.[1] Supporters of euthanasia may think it specious and legalistic to insist that in such a case relief of suffering is the direct intent and death an 'unintended' consequence.

Death may be welcomed; death may be hastened; but death is not to be the object of the exercise. The reason why this distinction matters is not an absolute and legalistic principle that suicide is wrong and not to be allowed, but serious *practical* arguments that acceptance of euthanasia is too dangerous.

Just as Paul Badham acknowledges the dangers of slippery slopes without changing his mind, let me acknowledge without changing my mind that the law in the Netherlands as he describes it makes a serious responsible attempt to meet the dangers, laying down strict conditions for acceding to a patient's request to die. For the sake of the argument the first three may be accepted: the patient's enduring free determination; fully informed consent; and intolerable suffering. The fourth condition, the absence of reasonable alternatives, is more doubtful: the slippery slope starts here. If it were current orthodoxy that euthanasia is the appropriate answer, would alternatives be strenuously explored? If 'better end it' had been acknowledged to follow directly from 'I'm sorry: that's all we can do', the hospice movement might never have discovered how much can be done for dying patients.

Paul Badham rejoices in the advances in palliative care, even affirming that 'the case for permitting euthanasia is no longer as strong as it was'. But his emphasis on 'permanent and continuous sedation' as the alternative to suffering does scant justice to the emphasis hospices place upon physical, mental and spiritual care for the whole person. Hospice care has been able, for many patients, to revive the ancient idea of the 'good death', without heavy sedation. A recent attentive perusal of death columns has yielded a strong impression that the word found much more often than any other is 'peacefully'. Surely this is not generally the wishful thinking of bereaved relatives? It is misleading to say that most of us die *alone* in hospital beds: particularly not patients who are 'wired up to saline drips'. There is room at the bedside for both technical and pastoral helpers.

Public opinion is easily swayed by gloomy pictures of the present and rosy hopes for kind permissiveness. But if the case against euthanasia is allowed to go by default, the cost of a 'better dead' presumption could be heavy.

Paul Badham takes trouble to be fair in balancing the fear of being legally 'put down' against the fear of doctors' wilful determination to fight 'a long-drawn-out battle against death'. He agrees that 'there is always a danger of sliding down slippery slopes', but his arguments take too little account of the longer run, and of the pressures on doctors and patients which could develop.

Doctors are for healing: it is not fair to ask them to abandon the tradition of the Hippocratic oath, which states that killing is wholly outside their role. At least, if we ask whether a doctor could ever accede to a request for death, we must not neglect to ask why it may be proper *not* to accede? 'Honour a physician with the honour due unto him for the uses that ye may have of him.'[2] Suppose these uses included being our executioner? The present state of the law lets us trust our doctors to combat our suffering even if the treatment also shortens our lives. The lethal injection is quite another thing. The distinction between killing and letting die is not 'arbitrary'. It is perilous to suggest that alongside the healing role 'a doctor might equally be seen as an agent of divine providence in bringing life to a peaceful end'.

Paul Badham does not quote Arthur Hugh Clough's 'New Decalogue'; but it is a pity to write off Clough's version of the sixth commandment as simply cynical. 'Thou shalt not kill, but needst not strive / Officiously to keep alive' puts in a nutshell the proper demand we may make upon the medical profession.

The pressures on the patient are just as dangerous. Paul Badham accepts that there is a real problem here and that liberal laws do not always have the results their proponents intend; but he does not adequately allow for the effect a changed climate of opinion might turn out to have. For the patient's firm wish for death it would be too easy to substitute the patient's feeling that 'It's time to go. It's selfish to hang on now that I'm only a nuisance.' Not all families are able or even willing to give their ageing relatives the strength of knowing that they are still valuable people.

Paul Badham sometimes lets his argument run away with him: for instance, the 'love and care' the Samaritans show is in *saving* people from suicide. When Job longed for death, we are told that he won through, not to euthanasia, but to a vision of God.[3] But still there is a great deal here with which one can warmly agree: the denial that all aspects of life are under 'the direct and immediate control of God'; the conviction that a 'good death' is something we may rightly hope for; the insistence that suffering is not good for us nor necessarily ennobling; the emphasis throughout on the Christian hope for life after death; the refusal to believe that the Father of Jesus Christ would damn a suicide as a deserter. When the argument slips into special pleading or overstatement, suggesting that suicide can actually be 'an affirmation of faith, hope and love', it is generous-spirited overstatement.

Notes

1. *The Times,* 29 October 1997.
2. Sirach 38:1.
3. Job 38ff.

Response by Susan F. Parsons

Paul Badham seeks in his piece on voluntary euthanasia to argue that, with a framework of clear guidelines and limitations, it is appropriate for a Christian to 'request the termination of his or her life' and for Christian doctors 'to accede to such a request'. Badham emphasizes that he means 'believing and practising Christians'. Thus he is concerned to demonstrate that the practice of voluntary euthanasia is 'legitimate', by reference both to biblical texts which are quoted as precedent, and to theological reflection upon the meaning of death and our responses to it. He seeks to assure the serious Christian that there is nothing here which is blameworthy before God, and therefore that Christians need not feel guilty for approving of, or assisting in voluntary euthanasia. Indeed his own piece suggests that it is right for Christians to go further than this, and to press the case forward legally following the Dutch precedent, so that voluntary euthanasia becomes permitted in British society too. Badham puts his case bravely, recognizing a huge weight of Christian tradition and opinion against him, and his piece is certainly timely in that the matters of despair and of hope in which his discussion is entangled are among the central issues of our time.

There are however several moods in his piece which disturb me, and which cause me both to doubt whether the case he hopes to press has been adequately upheld, and to wonder whether this is really the kind of argument that is the result of Christian belief and practice, or merely one which he thinks he can reconcile to his own Christian belief and practice. So there are weaknesses in his argument and, further, a sense in which I question whether its basic building blocks are intrinsic to Christian belief and practice. These two points are integral to one another.

The first mood which is striking and disturbing is the mood of individualism. In modern Western societies, we have come to accept as conventional wisdom that the most salient feature of our being human is our capacity for freedom, understood as freedom of choice, and that the high point of our personhood is realized in moral decision-making, when we choose between the alternatives laid out before us, taking a risk of action and bearing responsibility alone for our decisions. At these special and perhaps rare moments, our full personhood emerges and we are truly ourselves—courageous, lonely, authentic. That such freedom of choice might be removed from us is thus a major anxiety of our time, so that threats to personal autonomy are to be challenged wherever they appear, and a social order which can sustain the possibility for responsible individualism is to be sought. Is it any wonder that voluntary euthanasia has become an issue in this kind of moral world?

However, this kind of emphasis on individualism in the moral argument hides important features of our present situation, and I think in the end offers to us only an impoverished notion of personhood, inadequate to Christian belief and practice. What the picture of ultimately irreducible solitude misses is the sense in which we are entirely bound up within cultural conventions, a common language, and historical developments, from all of which we not only cannot extricate ourselves, but which give particular meanings to our decisions and actions. Without this broader context for consideration, this social body, we simply lose track of ourselves and are unable to account for what we do. And it is furthermore this context which provides a framework for critique, so that we gain some perspective on our personal choices and are challenged to deeper understanding and fuller growth.

Individuals considering voluntary euthanasia are not alone in their choices, or alone with members of their families and medical advisers. They are not persons primarily shaped by concern about limitation of their choices or intrusions of health-care professionals, as if the protection of these negativities could provide substance to their lives. Rather they are social persons, whose understanding of death has been culturally shaped by the practices of their society and the groups with which their own lives have been bound up. They are users of language within the fabric of which the rhythms of life and death are woven and their meanings given. They are products of particular times and movements of events out of which their lives emerge and to which they also will make contribution. All of these things make a difference to our consideration of voluntary euthanasia, such that we cannot rely upon the rhetoric of free choice and individual autonomy alone to sustain our moral lives and understanding.

Thus, we need to know about our society in which death has been pushed to the fringes of consciousness, being rendered very invisible close at hand and very visible at a distance. We need to know about the discourses in which we deal in death in our ordinary conversations and transactions, and of which our modern emphasis upon solitary individualism may be merely the latest chapter. We need to know about our history which reveals complicity in unprecedented destruction of human life, as though death were ours alone to manage, alongside burgeoning technologies endlessly multiplying the things of life that some can possess. In all of this knowing, we become aware of narratives of life and death in which we as individual persons feature, and the fullness of our personhood is somehow integrally related to our involvement, as one character or another, within these. There is no reference to these things in Badham's piece, so that it appears as a somewhat context-less disembodied argument, with a too-thin coating of pastoral insight and care.

Feeding and nurturing this individualism is a mood of discipline, a stern discipline which requires my self-assertion in the living of my life, as it requires my single-minded will in taking charge of my death. Badham's opponent in this piece is that opposition between life and death which, he claims, forms part of our cultural inheritance, in which death is thought to be some 'ultimate evil to be avoided at all costs', and the sanctity of life is believed to be some 'biblical absolute'. He wishes not to collude in these ideas, for they result in an ethical fundamentalism, a tidy world of moral clarity, in which they may be understood to yield unambiguous imperatives that lessen the risk of mistakes and protect us from our own moral blindness. Badham finds this approach unhelpful in investigating the complexities of issues involved in voluntary euthanasia, and in understanding the needs of those for whom it is a real and important consideration. His response is to reduce the differences between life and death, so that death is demystified as simply another event in the series which is life, and life is portrayed as actually not so wonderful in itself that it cannot be ended. Talking us out of the opposition is meant to aid a sober humane judgement.

In the process, however, it seems to me that we are being asked to support a willingness to be disciplined by death itself, such that the way we combat the notion that death is really a mortal enemy is to receive it willingly, to embrace its realities, and to take hold of its possibilities, at least insofar as these are rendered for our present understanding. Badham wishes to persuade us out of our fear, not simply fear of the unknown in the death that awaits us all, but more especially the fear of transgression, of stepping over that boundary into the domain overlooked by God's unforgiving countenance. To bring about one's own death, as suicide, has been understood to take one most particularly into that place, and thus it is an action which is hedged about with sanctions against despair. Against this, Badham urges us to recognize the ways in which a taking hold of our own death can be a way of fulfilling God's will, since human beings may after all also be agents of the divine providence, and of expressing a worshipful and prayerful anticipation of the promised life immortal. Turning to face one's own death reveals to us that, after all, this is not something which is so ultimately evil, nor is it something with which we are unable to cope, and so we may embrace it as the opening to new life. It is at this point that I wonder what story I am in.

I am left with a sense that, while ostensibly bringing death immediately before my awareness in the stark reality of its toughest implications and choices, nevertheless this is only a false death, and that somehow the real death's mystery has been even more heavily veiled behind words of human control of bodily pain and mastery of soulful despair. Badham draws from a particular strand of heroic philosophical thinking which insists that, while much of the junk with which I surround myself in daily living is entirely inessential to authentic life, my death, at least, is my own. It is my

taking death into my own hands in an assertion of my full humanity that will firmly establish my selfhood, so that I can stand with
well-deserved dignity before a divine demand for autonomous
actions, claiming rightfully that I did it my way. The remoteness of
the deity, indeed the absence of the deity, in this narrative reveals it
to be the endgame of the individualism of our time, and may go
some way towards accounting for the terrible lifelessness in
Badham's engagement with scripture.

The mood of individualism, along with its close and sustaining
relative of stern discipline is not, I believe, the one sustained by
Christian belief and practice. Rather it is the mood of our times in
the midst of which the Christian gospel is to be spoken and em-
bodied, and the task of this speaking and embodying is rendered all
the more awesome and all the more crucial by these cultural
moods, in the midst of which we are not brought in touch with the
divine love nor can we hear love's hope for the fullness of life. This
love is at once more challenging to our own understanding of ourselves and more appealing to the wholeness of our being than anything we can conceive by ourselves, as its hope is also more
challenging and more appealing to our true social being. Thus it
must be a real question for believing and practising Christians in
what sense the request to terminate one's life is a response to the
love of God, and once again I do not find reference to this in
Badham's piece. It strikes me that his is a piece which is weighed
down with death's judgement, in which he can argue about hope
without speaking words of hope, in which inattention to the social
body, most especially within the Church, hides from us the very
place of most concrete and specific engagement with this love and
this hope in the midst of Christian belief and practice.

Finally, because I do not believe that Badham's is a story of love,
it therefore places before me the hugeness of the work of pastoral
and medical care among the dying, a care in which persons may be
given space to grow in spiritual wisdom, not in the echo-chambers
of risk calculation, nor in the emptying of the heart until it can feel
no more pain, but a wisdom which is born out of the receiving
from, and the giving to God, of the love which is mine to know only

because it has been poured out for me, and which is mine to give only because I have been fully known. It is the silent holding of this space for others, and the spoken sustaining of this space with words of grace, which is the special privilege of care among the dying. It is this which many have known in hospice care, and which cannot be reduced, as Badham seeks to do, to the management of pain. For what remains is that which is most essential to the social embodiment of the gospel, namely that we are members one of another in a love that mysteriously and graciously and unendingly gives itself to us, and that to live with that love is to die with its hope scored deeply in our hearts. Only this can counter the morbid mood of individualism.

Response by Michael S. Northcott

The paper seeks to sustain three fundamental propositions: (1) The modern experience of death, dying and terminal illness occasions considerable and preventable suffering, suffering which is exacerbated by medical attempts to sustain patients who without medical intervention would die sooner. (2) A pro-euthanasia position is compatible with traditional Christian belief and ethics. (3) The modern utilitarian identification of moral agency with the capacity to suffer sets the moral good of the minimization of suffering above the good of the preservation of life. This prioritization requires a change in the law such that individual moral agents can assert this moral priority in the context of medical treatment for terminal illness.

In relation to proposition (1), Badham mobilizes a range of evidential statements which are very contentious. Thus Badham states that 'most of us will die alone in a hospital bed [so] wired up to saline drips and other support systems'. While it is true that 70 per cent of people in the United Kingdom die in hospitals or nursing homes, the claim that the process of dying is invariably medically extended, while it may be true in the USA, is not true in the UK. Badham asserts that most people live in fear of the agony of a long-drawn-out death and 'that doctors will fight over the battle-field of their bodies in defiance of their wishes'. In support Badham cites a study of death in the USA, a country which denies high-quality health care to the majority of its citizens, a country where people dread getting ill, to say nothing of dying, because it is the largest single cause of bankruptcy, and the first country in the history of the world to make the denial of death a cultural norm. While there is evidence from opinion polls of majority support for euthanasia in Britain, it is by no means proven that this is because the majority of people in Britain live in fear of a medically extended and painful death.

In the course of arguing for proposition (2), the harmonization of Christian tradition with the legalization of euthanasia, Badham asserts that 'the sanctity of life is not a biblical absolute. It is a value which has to be balanced against other values.' This statement is clearly untrue. Numerous passages in the Bible indicate that the shedding of blood is a serious issue because all living beings, and not just persons, are said to share the breath (*nephesh*) of the creator Spirit. In the Biblical perspective life is sacred, and it is this principle which underlies the sacrificial system and dietary rules in the Hebrew Bible, and the interpretation of the shedding of the blood of Christ at the Crucifixion as a salvific event in the New Testament, an interpretation which is most fully developed in the letter to the Hebrews though it also occurs in the Gospels and in the letters of Paul. It clearly is true that Professor Badham does not believe in moral absolutes, and that he prefers the concept of value—as an indicator of personal preference—to that of objective moral good, but to assert that there is no evidence for belief in such objective goods in the Bible is quixotic indeed, particularly in an article which professes to address 'Bible-believing Christians'.

This last error highlights a procedural problem. In the paper Badham claims to address 'Bible-believing Christians'. He uses the Bible in the way he imagines 'Bible believers' use it, as a quarry of proof texts which derive literal meaning from myth, parable, story and proverb without regard for literary or historical context, for the canonical location and shaping of the text, or for traditions of interpretation in the Church. Thus the Bible is said to support suicide because Biblical characters in the midst of violent conflict such as Samson, Saul, Avaran and Razis killed themselves (and their enemies in the case of two of them) rather than submitting to capture and death at the hands of their enemies. In using these examples as support for suicide Badham ignores the exceptional circumstance of war in which they occur, and discounts the clear teaching of Torah in the sixth commandment that the taking of life, including one's own life, is a violation of divine law, because it is a violation of the divine image in the human person.

Similarly in relation to New Testament evidence Badham proposes that the foundation of Christian ethics is the imitation of Christ. Christ himself is said in the Fourth Gospel to have chosen death. Christians who choose death are then imitating Christ. Once again a literalist interpretation turns the theological and religious shaping of the Johannine portrayal of the salvific death of Jesus into a Biblical warrant for suicide which is at variance with other explicit Biblical teaching, and most clearly with Torah, which in many of the New Testament writings is said not to have been abolished but fulfilled in the events surrounding the life and death of Jesus of Nazareth. The enthusiasm of some early Christians for martyrdom is also cited by Badham as evidence in support of suicide. But again contrary evidence in the tradition is ignored: Lactantius, Chrysostom and Jerome opposed the hastening of death whether for martyrdom or otherwise, and Augustine and Aquinas considered suicide contrary to the divine will. Church councils such as that at Carthage in AD 348 also condemned it.

The third proposition advanced by the paper—the moral priority of the minimization of suffering over the sanctity of life, and the necessity of a change in the law to reflect this new priority—is in fact the heart of Badham's argument. When we attend to the elements in the paper which advance this proposition, we see that (3) takes logical priority over (2) and furthermore that (2) plays only an illustrative and not a substantive role in the grounds for the assertion of (3). In other words Badham is advancing the case for euthanasia in classical utilitarian terms, terms which do not in any

way rely on the Christian tradition, or indeed make claims for
harmony with that tradition. This can perhaps explain why he is
prepared to use Christian evidence in such a partial fashion.

Once again, in advancing this third proposition, Badham makes
statements which are at best illogical and at worst untrue. Thus he
states that with the legalization of euthanasia 'medical intervention to actively bring about death may become less needed'. This is
clearly not so. Were euthanasia to be decriminalized, as it has been
in the Netherlands, doctors whose conscience permitted would
become involved in medical interventions actively designed to
bring death about. Currently it remains the case that doctors and
nurses involved in palliative care may offer pain relief to patients,
the secondary effect of which may be to shorten life, but their
active intentionality in so intervening is to relieve suffering, not to
bring about death. Badham's position appears to be that because
patients in the later stages of terminal illness may not be fully
informed about the possible life-shortening side-effects of a higher
dosage of painkiller, this means that these patients are effectively
being subjected to euthanasia without consent. The important
principle of double effect is clearly discounted by Badham at this
point. Doctors understand their primary goals in the management
of terminal illness as the minimization of suffering and the care of
the patient. The principle of double effect ensures that these roles
are not compromised by active intervention to hasten death. Most
medical personnel believe that their primary goals as carers will be
dramatically compromised by the additional optional goal of
hastening death, except where this outcome is a by-product of
a process of care whose primary goal is the preservation of the
dignity of the living patient.

This issue leads to the final problem with Badham's exposition of
his third proposition, and this is the extremely individualistic way
in which he conceives of the moral prioritization of the minimization of suffering over the preservation of life. The argument relies
at crucial points on the issue of patient consent. It is proposed that
the patient's wishes should be paramount, and in particular that
they should be paramount over the duty of the doctor to preserve

life, or at the very least not to directly cause life to be ended. However, this emphasis on patient consent ignores the relational context in which persons, including patients, live out their lives, and the relational character of moral goods such as the minimization of suffering and the preservation of life. In Christian ethics the presumption of not-killing has a range of grounds. It is an offence to God, as the originator of life, to kill a living person. It is also an offence to the category of persons for an individual or a society to permit killing, for when killing of any particular person is permitted the integrity of the generic category of person is threatened. And this is precisely the point that medical professionals make in opposing mercy killing. They argue that once the option of killing enters into the relationship of care, this undermines the moral goods which should be manifest in the caring relationship, such as trust, integrity, dignity, honesty, fidelity, love; goods which most living persons would wish to characterize the context of their own dying.

The utilitarian prioritization of the minimization of suffering over all other moral goods leads, as philosophers such as MacIntyre and Walzer have observed, to a very thin account of the moral life. This thinness means that utilitarians tend not to give due weight to the relational virtues which characterize medical professionalism and caring at its best. Badham discounts the possibility that the availability of euthanasia will lead to a diminishment of adequate palliative care. The empirical evidence also does not support his argument: palliative care is notably underdeveloped in the Netherlands, and highly developed in the UK. The heart of the problem is that the legalization of euthanasia will corrode the relationship between medical professionals and patients precisely because this relationship relies on moral goods and virtues which are discounted by thin utilitarianism, but which are central to accounts of the moral life advanced in Christian ethics.

Reply by Paul Badham

Response to Lady Oppenheimer

Lady Oppenheimer accepts the legitimacy of giving potentially lethal pain-killing drugs so long as the basic intention is to relieve pain and provided that death is not the object of the exercise but simply an 'unintended consequence'. She thinks this distinction is a 'proper use of casuistry' because preserving it enables the patient to be appropriately helped while at the same time preserving a bulwark against sliding down the slope 'which leads gently from the right to end one's life to the duty to end one's life, and so to the right or duty to end the life of someone we believe would be better dead'. She fears that this slide would occur if euthanasia were legalized in the UK, while I hope and believe that it would be resisted in Britain as it has been in the Netherlands.

My worry about being content to stop at the present British compromise is that it has a disturbing effect on the doctor–patient relationship. In a context where euthanasia is permitted, it is possible for all the issues involved to be thoroughly discussed between the patient, the family and the doctors, as happens in the Netherlands. But where euthanasia is forbidden the patient can have no knowledge of when, or if, the doctor will in fact implement a request for euthanasia by giving an overdose of painkillers which the doctor 'foresees' but does not legally 'intend' will kill the patient. The majority of doctors privately admit that they do help out patients in this way, but as long as the current law exists they cannot discuss their intentions with the patient, the family, the nursing staff or other doctors. The doctor has no choice but to make a lonely decision which may or may not be what the patient really wants. Hence the legalization of euthanasia could promote rather than impair the trust between doctor and patient.

By contrast with what is available to ordinary patients, Dr Michael Irwin, the former Medical Director of the United Nations, claims that 'many physicians and nurses have private arrangements that they will hasten each other's deaths should they ever be unfortunate enough to resemble the condition of some of their patients'.[1] In this situation trust exists, as it does in the Netherlands where it is common for terminally ill patients to secure an assurance from their doctors that they will euthanase them if they request it, but where few go on to ask that the request be implemented.

On the detail of my argument I do indeed see death as 'a positive good' when it is balanced against 'irreversible, protracted and unbearable suffering'. In my chapter I accepted that 'historically Jesus died a cruel death at the hand of his enemies'. My point was that under the influence of the Fourth Gospel, Christians have seen it as freely chosen, and indeed for the first 300 years of Christendom his example was cited over and over again as justification for volunteering for martyrdom. 'Volunteering' is the correct word since if one examines the records of Christian martyrs it becomes clear that 'very few were sought out by the Roman authorities . . . nearly twice as many (if not more) were volunteers'.[2]

Like Lady Oppenheimer I greatly admire what palliative care can do and she is right to point out that in recent years 'peacefully' has become the predominant adjective used in death columns. The macabre game of an earlier generation of counting up whether 'suddenly', 'peacefully' or 'bravely borne' was most common in the daily paper could not now be played. Yet although the situation is much better, agonizing and distressing deaths still do occur and it remains rare to find a death column which does not have at least some testimony to this. Whenever pain, suffering or an unacceptable level of dependency occurs in the dying process a small proportion of the dying will wish for medical assistance in ending it.

Response to Susan Parsons

I am puzzled about this response because I am much concerned for the social implications of what I discuss and what appals me about the present situation is the loneliness and isolation of a long-drawn-out death today. I see one very important gain in the allow-

ing of euthanasia to be that it would allow a person to die surrounded by love and care and with the support and comfort of the
Christian community. The importance of individual autonomy
was not a primary theme in my paper and indeed only in the penul-
timate paragraph do I discuss the primacy of free choice. In the
chapter as a whole as well as in my final conclusion it was precisely
the restoration of the Christian ideal of death as a communal
activity and as the gateway to a richer fuller life with God which
was my dominant concern.

I am sorry that Susan Parsons felt that I 'argue about hope without speaking words of hope'. This comment contrasts with Lady
Oppenheimer's observation about 'the emphasis throughout on
the Christian hope'. But clearly I should have been even more
explicit in speaking of the importance of our communion and
fellowship with God in the here and now which is the grounds for
our trust in eternal life with God hereafter. My whole approach to
the question of euthanasia is coloured by the fact that I believe in
the reality of life after death, and hence see no purpose in extending the agony of the dying process.

Response to Michael Northcott

Michael Northcott is robust in his critique but I do not think his
objections valid. Most authorities still show the majority of us
dying in hospital,[3] though I should have said 'many' rather than
'most' die wired up to support systems. Sherwin Nuland's book
How We Die documents in detail what it is like to die from heart failure, from cancer, from AIDS, from Alzheimer's disease and from
accidents or murder. That Nuland teaches in the Medical School at
Yale rather than in Britain does not invalidate his description, for
he is concerned with the human condition as such rather than
with the variations in health care in different countries. I accept
that the burdensome prolongation of life is more common in
America than in Britain, because our National Health Service
cannot afford knowingly to waste money on treatments which
have little hope of success, and because our law against trespass

gives us the right to decline unwanted interventions. But that the course of any terminal illness entails suffering of one kind or another is not open to question. It is the inescapable legacy of being human. Moreover, even in Britain the impact of much medical intervention is only to extend the dying process. That is the burden of the complaint against mainstream medicine by palliative care specialists. And even palliative care specialists witness to the inescapable suffering of terminal illness as they describe what can be done to mitigate it.[4]

Northcott may be right to say that one cannot actually 'prove' that the majority of people in Britain fear a medically extended and painful death. Recent research by Clive Searle has however shown that 28 per cent of relatives believe that it would have been better if their loved one had died earlier than they actually did.[5] One can also show that support for euthanasia is steadily growing in Britain: from 51 per cent in 1969; to 69 per cent in 1976; 72 per cent in 1985; 75 per cent in 1989; 79 per cent in 1993 and 82 per cent in 1996. This growth needs some explanation, as does the corresponding decline in those against euthanasia which dropped from 21 per cent in 1985 to 10 per cent in 1993.[6] According to Patrick Nowell Smith when President of the World Federation of Right to Die Societies, 'a large proportion of the people who join voluntary euthanasia societies' give as their reason for doing so that 'they do not like what they see in front of them in a society in which more than three-quarters of us will die in institutions'.[7] It seems reasonable to generalize that this also applies to those who have recently come to believe in euthanasia without necessarily joining a society, particularly as collections of essays on death and dying show how deeply embedded is the worry about the prolongation of life.

In my discussion of the biblical evidence I concluded that 'the sanctity of life is not a biblical absolute. It is a value which has to be balanced against other values.' Northcott asserts that this is 'clearly untrue' because numerous passages in the Bible assert that the 'shedding of blood is a serious issue'. I accept that the shedding of blood is a serious issue but do not see that this is relevant to my conclusion. Quite apart from the evidence I cited in my paper, the fact that the Old Testament Law prescribes capital punishment for so wide a range of offences (including adultery, homosexual intercourse, consulting mediums, insulting one's parents, and breaking the Sabbath)[8] suggest that from the perspective of the Hebrew Bible the preservation of human life is less significant than a range of other desiderata. Northcott himself acknowledges that war is an exception and this on its own would be enough to show that the sanctity of life was not a biblical absolute.

In my response to Lady Oppenheimer I discussed the way the imitation of Christ led Christians to a very accepting attitude towards death in the first three centuries. This is all very fully documented by Droge and Tabor in their work on *The Noble Death*. The examples that Northcott gives of the fourth-century reversal of this attitude by Augustine and others do not invalidate the point that the earliest Christians welcomed death whenever it came and indeed saw such an attitude as a corollary of belief in Christ's resurrection. According to St Athanasius all Christians 'treat death as nothing . . . they go eagerly to meet it . . . preferring to rush on death for Christ's sake rather than remain in this present life'.[9]

Northcott argues that where euthanasia is permitted palliative care does not develop. Like other opponents of euthanasia he claims that palliative care is 'notably undeveloped in the Netherlands'. But this is totally to misunderstand the Dutch situation. It is true that compared to the UK there are relatively few hospices or palliative care centres. But the reason for this is not that palliative care is not taken seriously, it is rather that it is taken so seriously that every hospital is required to have a special pain team so that palliative care is totally integrated into the operation of every hospital and nursing home. This is all fully documented in the encyclopedic survey by Margaret Otlowski which shows that, contrary to much popular belief, the permitting of euthanasia under strict conditions enhances rather than diminishes respect for human life, trust between doctor and patient, and the full availability of palliative care.

Finally, I turn to Northcott's theological objections to euthanasia, which I suspect are crucial to his whole approach. The central thrust is that God is the originator of life and hence it is an offence against God to kill a living person. I accept that the conclusion follows from the premiss. But just as almost all Christian married couples (including Catholics) now accept the legitimacy of seeking partial control over how life originates by using birth control, so it is not surprising that between 73 and 80 per cent of Christians would now like to take partial control of how their lives end through euthanasia.[10] As Hans Küng has pointed out, very similar arguments are employed in the Papal Encyclical against euthanasia (*Evangelium Vitae*) as in the Papal Encyclical against birth control (*Humanae Vitae*).[11] I believe that the two encyclicals stand or fall together. And just as almost all Christian leadership outside the Vatican has reluctantly come to terms with birth control, so sooner or later will Christian leadership have to come to terms with death control.

Notes

1. *Sunday Times*, 20 July 1997.
2. Arthur Droge and James Tabor, *A Noble Death* (San Francisco: Harper, 1992), p. 154.
3. See, e.g., Margaret Otlowski, *Voluntary Euthanasia and the Common Law* (Oxford: Clarendon, 1997), p. 449. Paul Ballard, 'Intimations of mortality: some sociological considerations' in P. Badham and P. Ballard (eds), *Facing Death* (Cardiff: University of Wales Press, 1996), pp. 14–15.
4. Illora Finlay, 'Ethical decision-making in palliative care: the clinical reality' in Badham and Ballard (eds), *Facing Death*, pp. 71–2.
5. *Times Higher Education Supplement*, 6 January 1995, p. 16.
6. The figure for 1969 is cited from the research of Patrick Nowell Smith (see footnote 7). The figure for 1996 comes from a letter to *The Times* by John Oliver on 1 December 1997. The remaining figures come from Otlowski, *Voluntary Euthanasia and the Common Law*, p. 259.
7. Patrick Nowell Smith, 'The right to die' in Paul Badham (ed.), *Ethics on the Frontiers of Human Existence* (New York: Paragon House, 1992), p. 211.
8. Leviticus 20:6–13; Numbers 15:32–36.

9.   St Athanasius, *On the Incarnation*, chapters 27–29: trans. by a religious of CSMV (London: Mowbray, 1963), pp. 57–9. For other instances see Droge and Tabor, *A Noble Death*, chapter 6.

10. Seventy-three per cent represents support for euthanasia among Roman Catholic laity and 80 per cent is the Anglican figure. Both cited in Otlowski, *Voluntary Euthanasia and the Common Law*, p. 259.

11. Hans Küng and Walter Jens, *A Dignified Dying* (London: SCM Press, 1995), p. 119.

Section 3

Euthanasia and the principle of justice

ALASTAIR V. CAMPBELL

Introduction

This paper is written from the perspective of clinical ethics. In it I am attempting to relate my experience of offering ethics consultancy in hospitals both in New Zealand and Britain to the theoretical debate about euthanasia. Thus I will begin with one person's story, and later I will introduce another. My aim is to test assertions about the rights and wrongs of euthanasia against the clinical demands of decisions in individual cases. I do not claim this to be the only, far less the normative way of resolving the problems, but I think that much of the discussion does lack the reality of clinical experience, and therefore tends to simplify or even caricature the real situations which people face in medical dilemmas about life and death.

Six and a half years ago I met a woman called Anna for the last time. Anna asked me to tell her story whenever I could, and I often have since that time. She was a woman in her thirties who was tetraplegic as the result of a road traffic accident some years previously. She also suffered diffuse phantom pain, which required constant administration of high doses of analgesic to make it bearable. Anna was married and had three young children. She had previously been a very active person—she had loved hiking and was an amateur singer of considerable talent. She also enjoyed amateur dramatics. By profession she was a schoolteacher. Now she felt she no longer had a life to live, that she was no longer the person she had been, and she wished to die. Although she had made it clear that she wished no resuscitation, she had suffered a respiratory arrest while away from her usual carers, had been resuscitated, and was now respirator dependent. After some months of discussion and the seeking of legal and ethical opinion, it had been agreed that her request to disconnect the respirator could be agreed to. A device was fixed up that enabled her to switch off the machine, and three days after our conversation, at a pre-arranged time and with all her family present, she flipped the switch. Drugs were administered to alleviate any respiratory distress and she lapsed into unconsciousness. However, a short time later she woke up and asked angrily 'Why am I still here?' More medication was given and she relapsed once more into an unconscious state. It was some hours later before eventually her breathing ceased entirely and she died.

It is situations like Anna's that lead to calls for a change in the law to legalize euthanasia. She *wanted* to die; her professional carers and her family knew this was what was sought in the discontinuation of the life support. Why then could she not have been killed more quickly and effectively by lethal injection, and without the long delay and debate which allowed the machine to be switched off? Moreover, since she did not die as a result of the treatment discontinuation, but only after more administration of drugs, was there not a dishonesty in claiming that this all fell within the range of legally permissible treatment? Was this not in reality 'physician-assisted suicide' under the guise of the legally allowed measures of refusal of treatment and relief of pain and distress?

In this paper I shall be arguing from within the perspective of Christian ethics, since that is where my own moral understanding is rooted, but the intention of my paper is to provide a foundation for the formulation of public policy within secular or religiously plural societies. I believe that 'natural law' can be described and illuminated from a Christian understanding of our obligations to our fellow humans. Let me describe from the outset the conclusion I shall reach: despite my sympathy for Anna, despite the problems which the current law causes for people like her and for those who care for them, and despite the moral ambiguities in interpreting that law in a way which is compassionate to those with irremediable suffering, justice requires that we do not change the law. To establish this conclusion I shall be trying to clarify the different kinds of decision which are taken in current medical practice, and of course I shall have to explain what I mean by the phrase 'justice requires'!

Decisions for the non-competent

I begin my exploration of the issues by considering a situation very different from Anna's. Right up to her death Anna was a very articulate person, clear in her own views, and insistent on having them heard and respected. A strong memory I have of her (captured on videotape) is of her interview with me in front of a class of nearly 200 medical students. The strength of her conviction that her life was no longer worth living, but that she was not merely temporarily depressed, carried a powerful authority, and made many of the comments given to her by well-meaning students about holding on to hope and considering her family hollow indeed. But we must note that much of medical practice does not hold out the possibility of this kind of dialogue with a competent patient seeking her own death in a reasoned manner. Many, perhaps most, of medical decisions about life and death need to be made on behalf of persons who cannot express any wish, either because they have not yet developed the capacity to formulate wishes and intentions, or because that capacity has been destroyed by illness or accident. It is important to look at this aspect of decision making—sometimes called non-voluntary euthanasia—before discussing the requests of competent persons for life-ending measures. The law puts boundaries on these decisions on behalf of others, which would remain—at least in theory—even if voluntary euthanasia were legalized. What is the justification of these boundaries? Let me again refer to a case of which I have had direct experience, to explore this question.

Zoe was born three weeks premature, had to be resuscitated at birth, and was admitted to an intensive care nursery and put on ventilator support and gastric feeding. It soon transpired that she had a rare but very serious inherited disorder, which had not been diagnosed prior to her birth, which involved a constant breakdown of her skin, both externally and internally.

Any contact with the skin surface could easily lead to large and painful lesions requiring persistent attention to bring about healing. The condition cannot be cured, and although the literature contained pictures of children who had survived three or four years their bodies were a mass of sores and their lives had to be so restricted physically that a normal childhood was impossible. The fact that Zoe had been intubated at birth meant that there was very likely already damage to her trachea, which would be prone to infection, and every intrusive measure entailed in providing neonatal intensive care (of which there are many) was very likely to cause further internal or external skin lesions and the associated pain and risk of infection.

Following full discussion in the neonatal team, and with Zoe's parents, it was decided to remove all forms of artificial life support from Zoe, but to maintain fluid balance and to try bottle feeding. As it turned out, Zoe was able to breathe without ventilation and she was moved to a side room outside the neonatal environment where her parents could easily stay with her. It was also decided not to treat any infection but to provide medication only for the relief of pain and distress. Zoe died six days later, probably as the result of an infection started by damage from the intubation at birth.

The same logic can surely be applied to Zoe as was earlier applied to the death of Anna—why a prolongation of six days, when a lethal dose could have ended things in a matter of moments? Of course, Zoe's wishes could not be known as Anna's were, but the potential for physical pain was much higher in Zoe's case—every act of touching was a risk. (In fact the nurses and parents felt sure from her reactions *after she left the high-tech area* that she was not in pain or distress and they learned how to hold her with care and tenderness without doing further damage to her skin.) The law did not allow the medical team to kill Zoe, but it did permit decisions to withhold treatment, some of it certainly life-saving, if such measures were judged not in the patient's best interests. But is the distinction drawn by the law a coherent and morally justifiable one? Or is it, as advocates for euthanasia argue, a piece of sophistry allowing doctors to kill patients under the guise of treatment decisions?

This is the issue which must be resolved before we debate the request of a competent person to be killed. It is evident that advocates for voluntary euthanasia (like Peter Singer and Helga Kuhse for example) are not simply arguing about honouring the wishes of the competent. In *Should the Baby Live?* they seek to demolish any argument that would draw a boundary between non-treatment and killing of neonates[1]—and the same must surely apply to the non-competent adult. From the consequentialist perspective of these authors the only relevant factor is the outcome of medical action or inaction. Thus if the death of Zoe can be predicted as likely when active treatment is withheld, then non-treatment must be the moral equivalent of killing if all other factors are to be discounted in the moral equation. Only consequentialist arguments are to be allowed in opposition to active killing, for example, arguments about creating a sense of insecurity in a society in which the incompetent can be killed if their lives are thought to be not worth living.

But we need not buy into the consequentialist assumption that outcomes alone have moral significance. This is a minimalist morality of a kind that ignores both the intentions of the relevant agents, and the social context of the choices which are being made in the course of a person's medical treatment. When we consider the care provided to Zoe, there is a universe of difference between the struggle to provide appropriate care, and the resolve to avoid meddlesome medical interventions on the one hand, and a decision to end her life expeditiously with a lethal dose on the other. The social context of the care of Zoe is one in which the values must always be biased towards the treasuring of life in the most fragile of circumstances—this is the essential philosophy of neonatal medicine. That treasuring must always be moderated by concern to ensure a peaceful death when efforts to ensure an endurable survival are proved to be vain. It is this subtle balance which is maintained by a legal framework which forbids killing but permits the withholding or withdrawal of treatment. To abandon this distinction in the name of a rationality which measures only consequences of actions is a denuding of the moral context of medical care. In the uncertain world of clinical care, the intentions and value orientations of those who provide the care are of fundamental importance, since they provide the barrier against the modern tendency to look for quick solutions to the moral ambiguities of our human vulnerability. The decision to give up on the survival of a person who cannot speak for herself should always be a hard and uncertain one. No law should make it easier.

Defining voluntary euthanasia

Having set the context of maintaining a distinction between killing, and withholding or withdrawing treatment from the non-competent, I shall now return to Anna's story. The events leading to her death are a good illustration of the continuing relevance of this distinction to the debate about legalizing voluntary euthanasia. When voluntary euthanasia Acts or Bills are framed there is a tendency to emphasize the agency of the person making the request, and to avoid reference to the fact that the proposed law will authorize an act of killing by another person. Thus, for example, an Act recently passed in the Northern Territory of Australia (but then struck down by the federal parliament) used the phrase 'assist me to terminate my life'. This seems to be referring only to decriminalizing counselling or abetting suicide, but in fact the administration by a doctor of a lethal substance was authorized by the legislation. It is dishonest to conceal the decriminalization of homicide in euthanasia legislation by using phrases which obscure the fact of killing. I therefore suggest that we describe voluntary euthanasia legislation in the following terms:

The object of the legislation is to decriminalize the killing of one person by another, under specified circumstances which include the competence and mental state of the person making the request to be killed, independent assessment of the medical circumstances which have led to the request, and the registering of the identity and the professional qualification of the person carrying out the killing.

On the basis of this definition we can see that Anna's dying encompassed a number of separable moral issues. The first was her request for no resuscitation and her later request to have the ventilator switched off. These seem clearly to be refusals of apparently life-saving treatment by a competent person, and such a refusal is clearly sanctioned by law in many administrations. (In New Zealand where the events occurred such a refusal of treatment is enshrined in a Bill of Rights.) The moral basis for such a legal right is that a person's liberty to decide what should be done to them by others cannot be constrained by arguments that others know better than they do what is best for them. (It is the same argument which allows a competent person to decide to commit suicide without criminal penalty, though attempts may be made to prevent the suicide in order to ensure that this is a considered decision.)

But Anna's later request entailed more than simple refusal of treatment. As a tetraplegic, she had virtually no freedom of action, but she wished to take an active part in disconnecting the ventilator. By devising a trigger which she could operate, the medical staff may have participated in physician-assisted suicide. Certainly this is how Anna perceived it, though in fact the disconnection did not result in her death. It could be argued, however, that the doctors were simply assisting her to implement her refusal of treatment, a very different situation from hooking her up to a Kevorkian-style death machine.

But the final complication came when Anna woke up off the respirator to discover that she was still alive. The administration of drugs at this stage seems clearly to be a response to her request to die, through ensuring that her still active respiration was further compromised. At this stage, in my view, the doctor killed the patient at her request, clearly an act of voluntary euthanasia as I have defined it, and therefore a criminal act, since there was no law to authorize it. No action was taken against the doctor in this case, nor was it likely to be given the circumstances of respiratory and emotional distress in which the sedatives were administered. But why should the doctor have to run such a risk of legal action? Why should voluntary euthanasia not be legally permitted, within a protective legal framework, to allow people like Anna to have their wishes met without jeopardizing their doctors?

The appeal to autonomy

I have now come to the stage of my argument where I must consider whether the request of a competent person for euthanasia
makes a significant moral difference to my earlier objections to
medical acts of killing of the non-competent. The moral argument
for voluntary euthanasia legislation appears to be mainly based on
an appeal to the principle of autonomy, namely, that since people
have a moral right to make decisions about their own lives, the law
must respect that right and not put obstacles in the way of their
decisions to end their lives with the assistance of others. But is it
clear what is meant by 'autonomy'? The term has a range of
usages, of varying 'thickness' or 'density'. A skeletally thin view
equates it with unqualified libertarianism—each individual should
be free to do what he or she pleases, provided that causes no
demonstrable direct harm to others. A somewhat thicker view
notices the *nomos* (law) component of the term, and argues that
individual values, life plans and considered decisions should be
respected—respect for the self-governing moral agent, and a commitment to help others discover and adhere to what Charles Taylor
has called their 'strong evaluations';[2] thicker still is the Kantian
notion of a 'rational kingdom of ends', in which moral agents all
voluntarily subscribe to the same moral laws, since these equate
with their shared rationality. I regard Kant's 'kingdom of ends' as
both unattainable and undesirable. There will always be a plurality
of moral views in any free society, and attempts to argue otherwise
lead to an authoritarian state of either a secular or religious type.
There are plenty of instances of such states in our recent history.

I believe, however, that we must, however difficult it may be,
retain something of the *nomos* of autonomy; we must look beyond
the fiction of isolated, individual choice and ask what effect granting such a choice will have on the community's values and on the
liberty and welfare of all persons in the society. I should stress that
this objection to euthanasia is different from the simple 'slippery
slope' type, which argues that any relaxation of the law will
inevitably lead to killing without consent. My interest is rather in

what legalizing voluntary euthanasia will entail for our concept of a just society in which the rights of all are protected, but in particular in which the vulnerable are not exploited. I am concerned both with the exemplary function of the law and with its power to protect all members of society, not merely to implement the wishes of the powerful and articulate.

What does justice require?

It is for this reason that I have referred to the 'principle of justice' in the title of my paper. In framing my title I had in mind the 'four principles' approach of Beauchamp and Childress,[3] and my argument is that eventually the issue is to be resolved not in terms of autonomy, beneficence or non-maleficence, but according to criteria of justice. Seeking legislation which is just takes us beyond individual choice to questions of the rights and welfare of all. If extending individual autonomy hazards the rights of others, then it cannot be the unquestioned basis for a change in the law. Of course there is much debate about what is required to ensure just laws. Some would argue, in the style of Nozick,[4] that it is to be equated with minimal interference in individual liberty (and this I take to be the basis of the 'secular bioethics' of Tristram Englehardt, to which I shall refer shortly). I shall not attempt in this paper to argue for the alternative to libertarianism of this type, but merely state that I am proceeding on the assumption (most fully spelled out by Rawls[5]) that an adequate theory of justice must balance individual liberty with equality before the law, and that our social arrangements must ensure an equality of opportunity and a maximization of the welfare of the disadvantaged. I regard this formulation of justice as closest also to a Christian vision of the just society, in which the poor, disadvantaged and vulnerable members become the central focus of concern. In this (no doubt socially radical view) majority benefit can never be used as a justification for disregard of those who cannot safeguard their own welfare; and individual liberty cannot be used to authorize the disregarding of the civil rights of all.

From this perspective there are three hazards to justice in legalizing euthanasia.

The first is to the moral framework of the community as a whole,
and of the medical profession in particular. I have already referred
to this in my discussion of the care of Zoe. The law against homicide serves as a reminder in the medical context of the precious
nature of every human life, and so requires a style of medicine
which finds the most caring solution to intractable suffering within
the boundaries of the legally permitted. In this way, the healing
ethos of medicine is maintained. But it is not only the medical context which would be affected. A law authorizing homicide would
send a powerful message about the fundamental values of the
society which permits its enactment. To many people the taking of
a human life in war or as a punishment for crime is already morally
repugnant, and campaigns are waged to bring about the peaceful
resolution of international conflicts and to abolish capital punishment. Euthanasia legislation goes in the opposite direction, adding
a new form of legal killing, and in doing so it also adds to the many
functions and powers of the medical profession the authority to
kill. It is essential to consider whether such an extension of power
over human life and death, even at the request of the individual
concerned, is something which our societies wish to sanction. It
represents a major shift in moral value, but one which might pass
unnoticed in the midst of the rhetoric of advocacy for euthanasia
in which the fact of killing is concealed by circumlocution. Grisez
and Boyle pose the issue of fairness to moral sensibilities as follows:
'How can a policy be regarded as liberal if it facilitates the liberty of
some citizens to kill and be killed by involving in activities repugnant to many citizens the legal processes and institutions in which
all participate willy nilly?'[6] This is certainly not a conclusive argument, since in a democracy with pluralist values there will always
be legislation which offends the moral sensibilities of some—laws
permitting abortion or homosexual acts between consenting
adults are obvious examples. My point, however, is that this question needs to be fully aired in the debate and not concealed by
implying that no more is at stake than the right to suicide.

A second area of hazard arises from the difficulty in defining the boundaries of the authorized killing. Let me stress again that this is not a 'slippery slope' objection. Rather it is an observation that the logic of voluntary euthanasia cannot be restricted to terminal illness as is sometimes implied. (Anna provides a good illustration of this point.) Whose judgement should it be that the reasons for a request are persuasive, and that, as the term 'euthanasia' implies, it is simply a question of easing an inevitable and proximate death? Any examination of the phrasing of euthanasia Bills will reveal the wide divergence in approach on these matters.[7] What of an incurable illness which may not result in the death of the patient, but which the person finds to be intolerable? (Many neurological disorders are of this type, e.g. multiple sclerosis, cerebral palsy.)[8] It soon becomes clear that the notion of terminal illness is irrelevant, and that the essence of any legislation must be removing the legal sanctions both against assistance to suicide, and against the killing of another, when that person wants to die and is not clinically depressed or otherwise mentally incompetent.

Such extensions to voluntary euthanasia may seem only logical, once legislation for the terminally ill is enacted, but they are also full of danger. We know from those who have been rescued from suicide attempts that many subsequently are glad to be alive, and find new ways of dealing with what at the time seemed intolerable. A person may be very vulnerable for a time without being diagnosable as clinically depressed. Thus this law could be a major hazard to the rights and welfare of the many people who will have to face periods of considerable ordeal in their life. Justice would therefore not be done to those individuals—it could be any of us—who come to periods of their lives when the burdens seem too great and the challenges to cope are hard to face. Can we really phrase legislation which allows such fine discrimination between justifiable and unjustifiable homicide on request?

The third, and in my view, most serious threat to justice comes from the synchronicity of debates about health care rationing, and debates about legalizing euthanasia. Because of the escalating costs of health care, the older age group, especially those with few material resources, are increasingly coming under threat by a society which emphasizes productivity and wealth creation. As the proportion of the elderly increases in societies which have experienced medical 'success', so the resources available for their treatment and care become reduced, and increasing efforts are made to recoup from the elderly themselves the costs of their care.

What is the effect of the legalizing of euthanasia on this group? It gives them another option. They do not need to feel a 'burden' on society any longer, nor need they fear that their last illnesses will deprive their families of goods they would rather their children enjoyed after their death. What was canvassed as a voluntary choice must surely be seen now as the responsible, loving and sensible solution to the problems which worry the more caring of the elderly. Voluntary euthanasia becomes the equivalent of the walk into the wilderness of the elderly of other societies. Regarding oneself as a burden which must be quickly and quietly removed becomes a sanctioned moral choice.[9]

This conflation of health care rationing and euthanasia is quite explicit in Englehardt's discussion of euthanasia in *The Foundations of Bioethics*. His starting point is what he calls 'secular bioethics', by which he means the only bioethics possible in a secular pluralist society which has minimal moral consensus. In such a society, Englehardt argues, 'the central . . . moral evil in murder is not taking the life of an individual, but taking that life without the individual's permission'.[10] It follows that voluntary euthanasia is morally acceptable, but Englehardt goes further, suggesting that it could also be a duty. He writes: 'One might imagine a patriotic citizen with a debilitating terminal disease committing suicide in order not to encumber further the Medicare fund.'[11] This leads on to Englehardt's prediction of what the future secular society will be like:

In a world of scarce resources and expensive technologies, it will appear only too reasonable that one should treat maximally and then freely effect death when treatments fail and pain and suffering become intolerable. Such will become the most reasonable secular use of resources . . . there will be immense pressures driven by economic concerns and fears of pain

... that will make ... euthanasia as reasonable and acceptable as prenatal diagnosis and abortion.[12]

If Englehardt's predictions are correct, then the use of 'voluntary' in euthanasia will become more and more dubious as resources diminish. It is hardly necessary to point out that in such a scenario the poorest and weakest members of a society will be the most likely to feel that 'voluntary' death is the only option, since the rich will still be able to purchase whatever care resources they need. If this is intolerable from the perspective of a secular morality, it is doubly so from a theological perspective. In Christian belief, the poor and vulnerable are especially objects of God's loving concern, and all Christian action must be biased toward the 'option for the poor' that is at the heart of the Gospel. For these theological reasons, I would argue that Christians need to oppose euthanasia legislation, not on the basis of a sanctity of life doctrine, which may be difficult to defend in view of our acceptance of non-treatment decisions, but on the basis of a Christian understanding of the truly just society.

Conclusion

I conclude that the moral and theological case for voluntary euthanasia, although powerful in its appeal to individual choice, fails to see the complexity of the moral issues involved, and in particular is in danger of creating injustices greater than any currently experienced as a result of the legal sanctions against assisted suicide and homicide. Of the three hazards to justice I have described the most serious is surely the third. To ensure justice for the vulnerable in our competitive and acquisitive society, there have to be powerful bulwarks in the law which prevent exploitation of the weaker members. Once the boundary is crossed and killing on request is legally permitted, it is hard to see how we could ever ensure that social and commercial pressures do not define the 'volunteers'. One could make a health service so poorly resourced that euthanasia was indeed the sensible option, or one can hold on to the moral complexities of a law which forbids killing even on request, and respond to the pressure this maintains on our society to provide skilled, humane and appropriate medical care to all its members.

All this means that I have to say to the spirit of Anna (which is still very much with me) that I deeply regret the long struggle she had to get the peace she sought, that it was intolerable that her wishes not to be resuscitated were ignored, but that in a society which cares for the vulnerable, the dignity of her death should not be achieved by legalizing homicide. Her ambiguous death is a price she and her doctor had to pay to ensure the safety of the weakest among us.

Notes

1. P. Singer and H. Kuhse, *Should the Baby Live?* (Oxford: Oxford University Press, 1985), chapter 4.
2. C. Taylor, *The Ethics of Authenticity* (Cambridge, MA: Harvard University Press, 1991), pp. 14–19.
3. T. L. Beauchamp and J. F. Childress, *Principles of Biomedical Ethics*, 3rd edn (Oxford: Oxford University Press, 1989).
4. R. Nozick, *Anarchy, State and Utopia* (New York: Basic Books, 1974).
5. J. Rawls, *A Theory of Justice* (Cambridge, MA: Harvard University Press, 1971).
6. G. Grisez and J. M. Boyle, *Life and Death with Liberty and Justice* (London: University of Notre Dame Press, 1979), p. 169.
7. For example, the original draft of the Northern Territory Bill required that death be imminent within a specified period of time, but this (for understandable reasons) disappeared in the Act, which merely stated that there be an incurable illness which 'will in the normal course of events result in the death of the patient'. Similarly, the Dutch approach to euthanasia has moved beyond situations of terminal illness.
8. What about a person diagnosed as HIV positive, who finds the future uncertainty of his condition intolerable; or a person with an incurable psychiatric illness, who in a lucid period wants to prevent further onset; or a person who discovers the first signs of Alzheimer's, but is still mentally competent?
9. It may be said that legislation will ensure that all such choices are genuinely those of the individual, and that any evidence of family

pressure would prevent the authorization of the killing. But this is to look only at the most obvious dimension of pressure on individual decisions. What the change in the law will do is to communicate to this group of people a social value, one which is explicitly ruled out by current legislation forbidding both assistance in suicide and homicide. The law signals the moral beliefs of a society, albeit indirectly and clumsily. The signal to the elderly person (and to people with disabilities) is clear if the law changes: provided they can convince two medical practitioners that they find their condition intolerable and that they are of sound mind, then part of the new medical service to them is painless and instant death. I remain to be convinced that any framing of euthanasia legislation can avoid creating this new social environment. But such an environment is, I believe, a grave threat to justice for such vulnerable groups in our society.

10. H. T. Englehardt, *The Foundations of Bioethics*, 2nd edn (Oxford: Oxford University Press, 1996), p. 350.
11. Ibid., p. 351.
12. Ibid., p. 352.

Response by Karen Forbes

Professor Campbell aims to 'test assertions about the rights and wrongs of euthanasia against the clinical demands of decisions in individual cases'. This may not be the normative way of approaching such a debate; however, I agree that much of the discussion about euthanasia lacks the reality and therefore the immediacy and gravity of clinical experience. 'Individual cases' are what my colleagues and myself as clinicians are faced with, and upon which we must form our opinions.

Professor Campbell discusses the distinction between killing and letting die with reference to both competent and incompetent people, then the moral significance of actions, the appeal to autonomy, and finally justice as a powerful argument against euthanasia. I will comment on each of these issues with reference to my personal experience as a physician in palliative care.

Palliative care as the alternative to euthanasia

Palliative care professionals are often approached to offer commentary when the latest 'individual case' emerges into the public eye. Presumably their thoughts and opinions are sought because they care for people around the time of their death and are therefore deemed to have, if not the answers, at least well-thought-out opinions about the rights and wrongs of euthanasia. The World Health Organization has defined palliative care as being 'the active and appropriate care of patients whose disease is no longer curable. It affirms life . . . regards dying as a normal process . . . and . . . *neither hastens nor postpones death.*' Most professionals working within palliative care, myself included, agree with this definition and find it helpful; however, some argue that hastening death by allowing euthanasia should be a logical and humane extension of good palliative care.

There is already enough confusion among both lay people and some medical colleagues about the use of drugs given to control pain, other symptoms and distress, so that palliative care professionals have to have clear views about the aims and appropriateness of medical interventions and therefore also about euthanasia. However, all health care professionals look after patients who are dying, and surveys suggest that up to half of all doctors have been asked by a patient to end their life. The debate therefore will and must continue in the widest possible circles. The moment to define one's own views about life-ending treatment is not when faced with a patient asking to be killed.

Killing versus letting die

We health care professionals have all met people like Anna. And if we are honest, we have all been faced with situations where we wished for the patient's death as a blessed release, even with the input of skilled, multidisciplinary palliative care professionals. This is because we do not have all the answers and palliative care, even at its very best, does not stop people asking to be killed. I think it diminishes the enormity of the requests, and the bravery of those who make them, to say that no one needs to have pain; pain can be controlled by applying palliative care principles, and that therefore good palliative care is the 'antidote' to requests for euthanasia. Even Professor Campbell softened us to Anna's case, I think subconsciously, by telling us *first* about her pain, *then* her previous abilities and her disability following her accident.

I argue that it is unlikely that Anna wanted to die because of her pain, although it will have contributed. I think it more likely that she, like all the patients who have asked me to shorten their life, wanted to die because of dependence, a perception that this led to lack of dignity and an inability to accept her current life in comparison to her previous one. A patient-centred approach, with due regard to the individuality and sensitivity of the person, can help restore dignity in some, but not all, patients. Sir Kenneth Calman has suggested that quality of life is a measure of the gap between a person's expectations and their reality. Anna's expectation/reality gap was enormous; she felt her quality of life was that there was 'no life to live' and that therefore death was preferable.

Physician-assisted suicide?

Professor Campbell raises the question of whether Anna's death was due to physician-assisted suicide. I agree with him that it was not. She had stated consistently that she wished to die. However, while she was mentally competent, she was physically incompetent to enact her own refusal of treatment by switching off her ventilator. A switch was therefore designed which allowed Anna to discontinue her own ventilation. I wonder if this elaborate procedure was necessary. A doctor switching the ventilator off would have been honouring a competent patient's wishes to refuse treatment. The likely outcome was that she would die from her underlying condition; however, the cause of death would have been the underlying condition and not the doctor's actions.

At the point that Anna awoke, in distress, asking 'Why am I still here?' Professor Campbell feels she was killed at her request. I disagree. Drugs can and should be used to treat both physical and mental distress at the end of life. In someone who had been ventilator dependent, it is likely that Anna awoke feeling extremely breathless. Breathlessness and the associated distress are some of the most difficult symptoms to manage; often distress is relieved only at the price of sedation. In Anna's case this will also have depressed her breathing and therefore may have hastened her inevitable death. In my opinion, sedation was necessary and humane, and the doctor was adhering to the principle of double effect. The drugs given may have hastened her death, but were given with the aim of decreasing distress. The doctor did not, in my view, kill her.

Outcomes of medical inaction

It will therefore be obvious that I do not agree with those authors who argue that it is only the outcome of medical action or inaction that is morally relevant, so that to kill and to allow to die are one and the same thing. I agree with Professor Campbell that the intentions and value orientations of those caring for patients are fundamentally important and I suggest that the model of affirming life, while regarding dying as a normal process to be neither hastened nor postponed, is a useful one. There seems a certain arrogance in the underlying assumption that with medical action, i.e. treatment, people will live, and without treatment people will die, and that therefore to deny medical action is to kill. It is salutary to remember that usually it is the timing of the outcome, rather than the outcome itself, that is altered by medical action or inaction.

Autonomy

Those who feel that euthanasia should be an extension of palliative care could argue that it is a logical extension of a care package centred around an autonomous individual exercising their moral right to make decisions about the end of their life. I think this equates with Professor Campbell's 'thin' view of autonomy. The 'thicker' view, which is far more useful clinically, respects the *nomos* component of the term autonomy, with the needs and wishes of the patient as the focus of care, but placed within the context of the patient at the centre of a group of family or loved ones. Any decision made by a competent patient must have an impact on the small community around her, and thus on to the wider community in which she lives. She cannot be viewed in isolation. Within this context of 'community', of which the professional carers are a part, it should be possible to consider the appropriateness of interventions in the case of an incompetent patient such as Zoe, with regard to the autonomy and worth of all.

Justice

Professor Campbell's three threats to justice are all extremely relevant in my main area of practice, the care of patients with cancer. In the majority of patients, particularly the elderly, the treatment of cancer controls symptoms and prolongs life rather than effects a cure. What is the point then, of patients' ultimately unsuccessful struggle against cancer? It prolongs the period during which they have pain and other symptoms (that is, are suffering), which is undignified, uses scant resources and could be avoided by granting the patient's wish, at one of the inevitable periods of despondency, of allowing them to 'die with dignity'. I argue that 'the point' is that this period of time allows people to take stock, and to do things, say things, and see people that are important to them, and to prepare themselves and those around them for their death and for life without them. Having cared for such patients I think there is an inherent dignity in this 'struggle'.

I agree that if euthanasia was legalized the boundaries of the authorized killing would be difficult to set, and might be influenced by the rationing of health care resources. However, I think that the strongest argument against euthanasia is the message that this sends to society as a whole about the worth of human life. To so disregard the dignity and worth of a person as to kill her, even at her own request, diminishes the dignity and worth of us all.

Why 'a peaceful death'?

Euthanasia is often seen as an answer to painful death. We all fear death and our concept of death is that it is painful. Most people have not experienced dependency since childhood; however, we have all experienced pain, and therefore extrapolate knowledge of pain to knowledge of how we might react if we were dying—we presume in pain. The majority of people make such judgements when they are in good health about a theoretical possibility at some time in the future. The presumption is that life would not be worth living should illness, frailty or disability supervene. For most, however, life remains precious even when this theoretical possibility becomes reality.

There will always be a small number of people, like Anna, who seek euthanasia, 'a peaceful death', as the humane alternative for them. My clinical experience leads me to conclude that they will, and should, remain the casualties of a system that denies their right to be killed in order to protect society as a whole.

Bibliography

K. C. Calman, 'Quality of life in cancer patients—an hypothesis', *Journal of Medical Ethics*, **10**(3), 1984, 124–7.

Cancer Pain Relief and Palliative Care, Technical Report Series 804 (Geneva: World Health Organization, 1990).

B. J. Ward and P. A. Tate, 'Attitudes among NHS doctors to request for euthanasia', *British Medical Journal*, **308**, 1994, 1332–4.

Response by Patrick Richmond

I would like to thank Professor Campbell for his stimulating, sensitive and realistic paper. I agree with his conclusion that we should not change the law to legalize medical killing. I also think that he identifies significant hazards that should give pause to those sympathetic to legalizing euthanasia. However, I have two reservations about his argumentation:

1 Professor Campbell's attempt to defend a strong, moral distinction between withholding life-saving antibiotics from Zoe and giving her a lethal injection looks doubtful.

2 His three main reasons not to legalize euthanasia seem inconclusive. It therefore seems that he has not justified his statement that 'justice requires that we do not change the law'.

I will try to explain these reservations before suggesting a way in which his case might be strengthened.

(1)   Zoe: withholding treatment and intending death

Professor Campbell attempts to defend a strong, moral distinction between killing someone and letting them die. As he says, consequentialists like Singer seek to demolish any argument that would draw a moral boundary between non-treatment and killing. They point out that the outcome of both is the same, the death of the patient. They also note that lethal injection would cause the desired outcome more efficiently, without the risk of protracted suffering. It would remove the dependence on chance events, e.g.

infection, in causing the peaceful death believed to be best for the patient.

I echo Professor Campbell in rejecting a moral theory 'that ignores both the intentions of the agents and the social context of the choices'. However, consideration of intention *strengthens* the argument that non-treatment can be as bad as killing. In both non-treatment and injection the intention may be that the patient should die. If someone intends another to die, it does not excuse them if they brought that death about by deliberately withholding life-saving help rather than by killing. The decision not to give life-saving help is a mental act, not just an omission. For example, if I intended my baby to die, it would be no excuse that I achieved her death by deliberately letting her drown in the bath. The fact that I did not actively kill her would not save me from moral guilt. Consideration of intention supports the claim that withholding life-saving help can be morally similar to killing.

What about the context? The context is 'one in which the values must always be biased towards the treasuring of life in the most fragile of circumstances—this is the essential philosophy of neo-natal medicine . . . moderated by concern to ensure a peaceful death when efforts to ensure an endurable survival are proved to be vain'. Thus, sometimes, survival is judged unendurable. Singer gives examples of non-treatment of babies with severe spina bifida.[1] When one intends death, is the decision not to save life biased towards the treasuring of it? Even if it is, must this outweigh the concern for peaceful death so that slow death by infection is preferred to painless injection?

Professor Campbell then claims that 'The decision to give up on the survival of a person who cannot speak for herself should always be a hard and uncertain one. No law should make it easier.' Arguably, allowing the omission of simple, effective, life-saving treatment like antibiotics *does* make the decision to give up on survival easier; it distances one in time and space from the patient's death. It allows superficial differences between killing and letting die to obscure the fact that one's underlying intention in both cases is that the baby should die.

At this point I should mention a moral distinction that seems more defensible than that between acting and deliberately omitting to act. This is the distinction between the intended goal of a decision and the foreseen side-effects. It is central to Roman Catholic moralists' use of 'double effect' in justifying some decisions that bring about foreseen, and harmful, side-effects. For example, the Roman Catholic Declaration on Euthanasia in 1980 allowed the withholding or withdrawal of treatment that was disproportionately risky, costly, painful, or intrusive compared with its therapeutic benefits. Given such decisions, death might come earlier than it would if doctors treated the patient. However, the *intention* is to avoid unreasonable risk, cost, discomfort or intrusion. Earlier death is the foreseen side-effect. There is a judgement that a *treatment* is unreasonably burdensome. There is no judgement that the patient's *life* is unreasonably burdensome. In such cases the intention is different to that in euthanasia. This distinction also applies to active treatments, e.g. pain relief with harmful side-effects.

Professor Campbell may allude to this consideration when he talks of 'the resolve to avoid meddlesome medical interventions'. However, in Zoe's case this consideration does not explain the decision to withhold antibiotics. The antibiotics would be reasonably cheap, effective and painless. It seems it was not the antibiotics that the doctors judged unendurable; they judged Zoe's *life* unendurable. Although the nurses learnt to handle her so that she was 'not in pain or distress', a 'normal childhood was impossible'. I may be mistaken, but this decision seems based on ideas of an acceptable quality of life. Zoe's life was judged not worth living. Giving her antibiotics would have been 'meddlesome' only because she was deemed better off dead. The statement that 'a sanctity of life doctrine . . . may be difficult to defend in view of our acceptance of non-treatment decisions' strengthens suspicions that doctors intended Zoe's death.

Here I register my own unease about many judgements that continued life would be unendurable or not worth living. As Professor Campbell notes later, what someone can endure depends on many subjective factors. In many cases there seems no objective, rational way of calculating whether the value of a life outweighs the disvalue. There seems no objective scale on which the values and disvalues can be weighed.[2] A general refusal to countenance judging another person's life as not worth living also seems less judgemental and more generous, inclusive and humble. It coheres well with the principle of basic, equal respect for all people. I therefore query the objective rationality and social desirability of many judgements that others' lives are not worthwhile.

I conclude that Zoe's case is grist to Singer's mill. Consideration of intention shows that some non-treatment decisions and life-shortening treatments do not intend death. However, in Zoe's case, as in others, peaceful death *does* seem to be intended. Consideration of intention and context strengthens the suspicion that non-treatment here was no better than injection. Not only was the outcome substantially similar, so was the intention. Medics are already judging some lives not worth living. They are already intending that some babies die. The means used, deliberate non-treatment, serves to obscure the fact that death is the chosen end and makes the decision easier. Professor Campbell appears to leave his train of argument before it reaches its logical station.

(2)   Indecision: where to draw the line?

Early in his paper Professor Campbell claims that 'justice requires that we do not change the law'. Unfortunately he offers no undisputed principles of justice, the hazards he identifies are often already to some extent accepted by the legislature, and he neglects the hazards of not permitting euthanasia. His arguments therefore seem inconclusive.

When we read the section of the paper, 'What does justice require?' it is clear that the concept of justice is disputed. In his paper Professor Campbell assumes without argument that a more 'Rawlsian' concept of justice is to be preferred to a more libertarian understanding. This is problematic, since pro-euthanasia campaigners often have libertarian sympathies. Further, the Rawlsian view is 'no doubt socially radical'. It therefore hardly provides a secure premiss for argument.

Professor Campbell suggests that such a view is close to a Christian vision of the just society. Should Professor Campbell see such closeness as a sign of truth? He believes the sanctity of life doctrine, arguably important to Christian tradition, 'may be difficult to defend'. If he is prepared to abandon important Christian traditions then he cannot put much weight on the tradition as a guide to truth.

Even if we grant that the poor, disadvantaged and vulnerable are the focus of concern, are the hazards he identifies decisive? I see little argument that they are.

Take the risk to 'the healing ethos of medicine'. Professor Campbell already notes a significant qualification to this healing ethos in his acceptance of non-treatment decisions. This qualification is reinforced by the practice of abortion. What about 'the fundamental values of society'? Euthanasia affirms the values of mercy and autonomy. It is true that euthanasia legislation would create a new form of legal killing by the medical profession. However, legalized abortion already grants some authority to kill. Medics already have considerable authority over life and death. Nor is the prohibition on killing universal. Many people condemn war and capital punishment, but many defend them. What is more, suicide and the use of lethal force in self-defence can be legal, so all have legal permission to kill in certain circumstances. Finally, why must the moral sensibilities of some defeat the rights of the vulnerable to get the euthanasia they want?

Professor Campbell then points out the pressure not to restrict authorized killing to terminal illnesses. There is a risk that vulnerable people will commit suicide who might otherwise have recovered or learnt to manage. These are important points, but not conclusive. Risks could be controlled. Euthanasia societies in England have suggested that a diagnosis by two doctors of an incurable illness expected to cause significant distress or loss of rational faculties should be required.[3] Hasty decisions might be avoided by requiring a 30-day 'test' period before euthanasia.

Though a few might die unnecessarily, it would be their responsible choice, verified by independent witnesses. Conversely, many vulnerable people would be spared significant suffering. It seems suspiciously paternalistic to deprive them of this option to remove risk. After all, the law allows vulnerable people to take various risks with their lives, such as suicide, smoking and rock climbing. Why is this risk unacceptable?

Professor Campbell's 'most serious' point is that the poor and old will be pressured into euthanasia. The elderly will feel moral pressure to request euthanasia rather than be a burden on society or waste their family's inheritance. This pressure will be greater for the poor; the rich can purchase care for themselves. If this argument were decisive, it should forbid suicide and refusing treatment, for the poor might choose these actions to avoid wasting resources. However, society *already* allows suicide and refusal of treatment. Nor is it clear that outlawing euthanasia is the best 'option for the poor': if they consider life worth living then they will want health care; if they do not think that life is worth living then the law against euthanasia is unlikely to help and may even seem a paternalistic infringement of their liberty. The misery of those refused euthanasia is palpable. Legalization could prevent this prolonged misery for the poor as much as for the rich. Thus one might argue that guaranteeing the poor the care they want shows them more loving concern than refusing them euthanasia when they responsibly request it.

So it seems that Professor Campbell identifies real hazards, but fails to identify a clear line that should not be crossed. How might he strengthen his argument? He could draw the line at intending the death of innocent people. This position is no less plausible than 'Rawlsian' justice and has the advantage of clearly ruling out certain policies. Unlike just war, capital punishment, self-defence and medical decisions with unintended side-effects, euthanasia transgresses the line. Nevertheless, we must face the fact that our society may already have crossed it.

Notes

1. P. Singer, *Practical Ethics* (Cambridge: Cambridge University Press, 1979), pp. 131–4.
2. There may be an exception when there seems no possibility of value, e.g. in cases of persistent vegetative state. Perhaps an individual in a persistent vegetative state is no longer a 'person' in the morally relevant sense.
3. Singer, *Practical Ethics*, p. 143.

Response by Nigel Biggar

In spite of his protestations to the contrary, Alastair Campbell's opposition to the legalization of voluntary euthanasia seems at first to take the form of an enlightened consequentialism. He does not object to legalization on the ground championed by Germain Grisez and John Finnis—that any act of intentional killing, since it involves the turning of the will against the good of life, is malevolent and so corrupts the moral character of the agent. Nor does he oppose it (at least deliberately) by challenging patient autonomy in the name of a superior understanding of the patient's good. Instead, he argues against legalization because of its effects upon the moral climate of society as a whole and of the medical profession in particular, and thereby upon the protection of the vulnerable and poor. His argument turns on consequences.

It is true that Campbell takes pains to distance himself from 'consequentialism'. Against Peter Singer and Helga Kuhse he seeks to uphold the traditional moral distinction between the permissible withholding or refusal of life-saving treatment, and impermissible killing. He denies that outcomes are the only morally significant feature of an act, and insists upon the consideration of the intentions of the relevant agents and their social context, too.

Nevertheless, what he is really arguing for here is a broader and deeper understanding of 'outcomes'. For it is not that he regards any act of intentional killing, including those performed with the consent of the patient and motivated by compassion, as intrinsically evil. Rather, his concern is with the social effects of legalizing intentional killing by physicians. He sees law as having a symbolic, as well as a regulative, function. In addition to prohibiting or enjoining certain kinds of acts, it also symbolizes or represents corporate values. So the law against all forms of homicide represents the high value that society places upon the life of every human individual; and it thereby encourages an ethos in the medical and nursing professions that treasures human life. Campbell is arguing that, even though intentional killing of patients by physicians might seem morally right in certain cases considered apart from their wider social context, to make the law permit such killing would weaken the high esteem in which the life of the individual is generally held by doctors and nurses. In an economic context of escalating health-care costs, in a political context where the pursuit of ever greater efficiency in the use of resources is the response most popular with taxpayers, and in a cultural context that tends to measure the worth of an individual in terms of her productivity, the law's permission of physicians to kill consenting patients—or to help them kill themselves—would soon be read as society's encouragement of heavily dependent persons to do their duty, and relieve their families and taxpayers of the burden of supporting their rather worthless lives by seeking an efficient death. Such 'encouragement' would, of course, be felt more by some than by others: most acutely by the elderly and those dependent on state-provided health care, and least by those able to buy care out of their own resources. In sum, then, Campbell's main argument amounts to this: that to relax the law against homicide in order to permit physicians to kill consenting patients—not to mention giving patients the right to be killed or assisted in suicide—would have as its outcome a gross form of social injustice; and it would therefore be wrong.

At this point, of course, it becomes clear that the argument is not in fact consequentialist, for it employs a concept of justice. According to Campbell, the immorality of an act of voluntary euthanasia is certainly not established merely by its consequences for the patient; but nor is it established by the probability that it will harm more people than it benefits. Rather, it is determined by the probability that its legalization will result in the injustice of a widespread failure in the duty of special care for certain vulnerable classes of people. What qualifies the monopoly of moral significance claimed for consequences by consequentialists, then, is not so much the intentions of the relevant agents or their social context, but their duty to support the weak.

One of the greatest virtues of Campbell's argument is that it draws our attention to the social formation of the individual's autonomy—the social and commercial forces that help to determine 'volunteers'. A competent individual may really want to die. He may want to die because he is quite convinced that he should: he feels quite acutely that he is simply a burden and he is keen to cease being so. This is what he genuinely wants; this is his authentic will. If the autonomy of competent patients is held to deserve from physicians the respect of compliance, then such an individual's doctor should either kill him or help him to kill himself. But Campbell's line of argument leads us to scrutinize the notion of 'respect'. Would respect for individual autonomy in this case really be an act of care, or would it be an act of indifference—even of abandonment? Is it acceptable that someone should regard their own life as 'simply a burden', largely because that is how society rates it? Is it acceptable that society should rate it so? Should not society strive—not least through its laws—to reassure such a person and to affirm the value of his life? And might not his own will rise up, turn around, and embrace such reassurance with a deep sigh of relief and gratitude?

The point here is not that it is always impossible to distinguish the authentic will of the individual from the social forces that shape it; far less, that that will is reducible to such forces. No, the point is that what I genuinely wish is not independent of what those around me wish; and that sometimes I wish something that I would not, if those around me cared for me. Therefore, unless we are careless, we may not take the accurate expressions of a competent person's genuine will at face value. We must examine it to see whether or not it is significantly shaped by a failure of social support. Uncritical respect for autonomous wishes is not enough.

A second, closely related, virtue that characterizes Campbell's argument is its strong implication that the morality of an individual case cannot be established apart from consideration of its social context. His position is not exactly that a case where it would be morally right to grant a request for voluntary euthanasia should be trumped by considerations of social justice. It is rather that, in light of the requirements of social justice, both the request for and the practice of voluntary euthanasia in this case would be wrong. Here, the patient has a duty not to ask her physician to do something which, if legal and so generally permitted, would harm the respect and care given to the lives of others; and the physician has a duty, if asked, not to comply.

A third commendable feature is Campbell's contention that legally authorized voluntary euthanasia could not logically be restricted to cases of terminal illness if its main ground were—as it would likely be—respect for the patient's autonomy. For unless we were prepared to justify 'paternalist' contradiction of the express and considered wishes of a competent patient—or, indeed, simply a competent person—we could not rationally refuse a request for voluntary euthanasia from such a person just because *we* thought their life worth living in the absence of terminal illness.

Campbell himself, however, is equivocal on the subject of 'paternalism'. On the one hand, he appears to endorse (because he raises no objection to) a liberal justification of the legal right of a competent person to refuse apparently life-saving treatment or to commit suicide: namely, 'that a person's liberty to decide what should be done to them by others cannot be constrained by arguments that others know better than they do what is best for them'. This appearance is confirmed when he rejects the Kantian notion of respect for individual autonomy as subject to the moral laws of universal human rationality, and opts for Charles Taylor's thinner notion that we should respect whatever happen to be the 'strong evaluations' of autonomous moral agents.

On the other hand, Campbell points out the danger of permitting voluntary euthanasia to any competent person who requests it: namely, that those who are emotionally vulnerable but not clinically depressed (and therefore 'incompetent') will not be prevented from making an irrevocable decision that many of them, if prevented, would later recognize to be a grave mistake. The obvious implication here is that society, through its laws, should deny (at least some) competent patients the exercise of their autonomy in the name of their own best interests, which they currently fail to recognize but will come to recognize in time. This, surely, is an argument (and a cogent one) for some form of 'paternalism', and one that exposes again how liberal 'respect' for the autonomy of rational individuals can amount to careless abandonment.

In conclusion, Campbell's argument performs the good service of raising telling questions about the sufficiency of mere respect for individual autonomy, and of alluding to a distinction between careful and indifferent kinds of respect. Thereby, it also inadvertently suggests that there may be more to be said for a certain 'paternalism' than Campbell himself is yet willing to admit.

Reply by Alastair V. Campbell

I am grateful to all three respondents for the positive yet probing nature of their comments. It is interesting to note that often the most trenchant criticisms come from those who agree with your conclusions, but want to improve your arguments for them! This can often be a livelier debate than the simplifications that occur in the polarization of arguments 'for' and 'against' euthanasia. Where then are the weaknesses in my arguments against legalizing euthanasia, and can they be remedied?

Intention and double effect

First, there is the question of distinguishing euthanasia from permissible medical treatment by reference to intention. Karen Forbes argues that the actions of the doctor at the very end of Anna's life could be justified by the principle of double effect, the primary aim of the sedatives being the relief of respiratory distress. On this account, it is not necessary to describe what he did as 'physician-assisted suicide'. Patrick Richmond also appeals to the principle of double effect, in relation to the withholding of antibiotics from Zoe, but he argues that, since antibiotics are a straightforward, non-burdensome treatment, the doctors' intention must have been to end Zoe's life by an act of omission. He concludes that I am wrong to try to distinguish what happened to Zoe from euthanasia.

I suppose I am trying to stay in somewhat uncomfortable territory between these two views, finding the Forbes justification too easy, but the Richmond account of intention and of what is burdensome too restrictive. (This difficult middle position is hardly surprising, since I deliberately chose clinical situations which have, in my opinion, considerable moral ambiguity.)

Let me deal first with the question of culpable omissions, referred to by Richmond in his example of the parent allowing his child to drown in the bath. I accept his conclusion that this omission appears morally similar to killing, because it makes no sense to say the parent did not intend the death, when he knew for certain the outcome of inaction and was physically able to save the child. But it is possible to invent circumstances in which even this situation could be redescribed as allowing the baby to die as peacefully as possible through deliberate inaction, rather than as killing. Imagine that the bath is in the midst of a terrible house fire, from which the father has sought an exit in vain. If he pulls the child out of the water, she will almost certainly suffer excruciating burns, and will most likely die, if not soon, then after some weeks or months of misery. Is he morally obliged to risk these outcomes for the baby on the grounds that to fail to rescue her is tantamount to killing?

This imaginary example is not far removed from the decision not to intervene medically if Zoe got a lung infection, since the burden of pain and continued medical intervention till an early death was all too clear. Similar decisions are made about non-resuscitation after cardiac arrest, or non-treatment of pneumonia when patients are in the advanced stages of malignancy. These are judgements about the intervention leading to more burden than benefit, and the burden, I readily admit, relates not to the treatment itself but to the consequences of preventing an earlier death. I cannot see how we can escape making quality-of-life decisions of this kind, in circumstances when we cannot consult the patient, however difficult it may be to be sure that we have the calculation right. The alternative is to put the non-competent through treatment regimens which we can readily expect few if any competent patients to accept.

Richmond is probably right, however, that if we accept the validity of such quality-of-life decisions, whether by accepting the moral permissibility of refusal of life-saving treatment by the competent, or by taking non-treatment decisions on behalf of the incompetent, then we are going to find it difficult to oppose active killing in the same circumstances. In the imaginary situation above, why would pushing the baby under the water to save it from the pain of burning to death be any different?

Double effect justifications work only when we can make a clear distinction between one regimen which is obviously concerned with pain relief in commensurate doses and another which will kill the patient quickly, under the guise of pain relief. The emergence of palliative care as a specialty has allowed us to make these distinctions with increasing sophistication. But there are other circumstances when a decision not to treat or to withdraw treatment is, as Richmond observes, clearly related to the intention to end a life. This was the case with Anna's decision, and it was one which inevitably involved the doctors assisting her. When the respirator was withdrawn and she woke up, that joint decision that her life should end was frustrated. Forbes is in part right to say that subsequent medication was justified to alleviate distress, but she is also honest enough to say that often doctors fully support the patient's desire to die. I doubt very much that the primary intention of the doctors sedating Anna after her arousal was to alleviate respiratory distress, though one can see why they might wish to maintain that stance in view of the legal perils of admitting their real intention. The danger, however, is that such a dubious use of the useful principle of double effect can bring it into disrepute.

So I conclude from my responses to these commentators that indeed the ambiguity remains, and that we cannot defend all cases of treatment of distress and of non-treatment of patients with poor prospects as entirely distinct from euthanasia. The stringency of Richmond rules out too much good medical practice, while the liberalism of Forbes erodes the boundary with active euthanasia. I'm not convinced we can escape that ambiguity in clinical medicine, even though it occurs far less often than the rhetoric of the euthanasia lobby claims.

Justice, autonomy and paternalism

Perhaps, then, we can find a better distinction at the social and legal level, rather than at the clinical. Nigel Biggar correctly sees the importance of symbolic and social aspects of the law as the central argument of my paper. I am willing to concede the fuzziness of the boundary between active and passive euthanasia in some clinical situations, but I believe that active euthanasia should remain illegal on grounds of justice. The question is whether this argument carries sufficient weight. Forbes, on the basis of her experience with vulnerable people, believes that it does; Richmond wants to offer me a stronger argument; Biggar sees its force, but wonders if I have seen its full implications for my account of autonomy.

I must first stress again that my argument is not consequentialist, except in the extended sense suggested by Biggar of pointing to 'outcomes' of legalizing euthanasia. These outcomes are not, however, simply empirical predictions: they are, in my view, the logical outcomes of authorizing medical killing. My opposition to euthanasia legislation does not depend on a consequentialist calculus of the balance of predicted benefit and disbenefit, but rather on an account of unacceptable changes to our social values.

Richmond may be right to worry about the force of some of my arguments. It is true that my account of justice will have little effect on outright advocates for libertarianism, but then why should his alternative of a boundary against 'intending the death of innocent people' carry any more weight in a culture of individual competitiveness? Both he and I depend on a social consensus of a post-Christian kind that puts protection of the vulnerable ahead of aggregate social benefit, or of benefit of the socially advantaged. I also accept that the argument against offending moral sensibilities is persuasive merely, and, as I point out in my paper, it has certainly not been normative in other legislative changes. But I still want people to be aware of the values that are at stake, since advocates for euthanasia often present themselves as the only ones concerned about freedom and about the weak and vulnerable. I am disappointed that Richmond seems to go along with this idea in his suggestion that euthanasia could be seen as respecting the rights of the vulnerable. The whole point of my analysis is that this is an illusion, created by a minority of articulate people, who no doubt could exercise their right to choose their death more easily, but only at the expense of the rights of others.

Biggar perceives that I want to focus on the symbolic function of the law, and on the effect on social and cultural attitudes of a law authorizing killing as part of the range of professional health-care skills. This change in social context has a corresponding implication for how patients perceive themselves and so how their choices are shaped. Richmond suggests that voluntary euthanasia could be seen as on a par with suicide or refusal of treatment, both of which are legal. Why, he asks, are we entitled to decide that the poor (or the rich for that matter) must be denied the liberty of arranging to have their lives ended? Is not this a worse 'option for the poor' than giving them a new way out of their 'prolonged misery'? My response is that he appears to underestimate the effect of a law authorizing killing, as opposed to legislation which has decriminalized suicide and which prevents medical treatment being imposed on people against their will. Such a law would create a new option for those who felt themselves a burden, which would undoubtedly affect the poor unequally, because they would not have the resourses to meet the increasing costs of their care. In my opinion the dilemmas of rationing and of euthanasia are very closely related.

To what extent, finally, is my opposition to legalizing people's choice of euthanasia really a form of paternalism, as both Richmond and Biggar suggest? Am I trying to save people from themselves by blocking a law which could induce them to take a hasty and ill-considered exit? Biggar neatly captures the point I am trying to get across when he describes how respect for autonomy can amount to 'careless abandonment'. Should I then be more forthright in defence of paternalism, rather than equivocating, when it comes to rights to refuse treatment or the adequacy of Kant's account of moral autonomy? I don't think so. I don't really want to defend paternalism at all, even in quotation marks, as in Biggar's text. Perhaps this is largely a matter of semantics, rather than substantive argument. I understand paternalism to be the *unjustified* use of personal, social or professional power to make people conform to what one perceives as their best interests. I do not have the certainty about moral laws that could lead me to prevent people from making choices about what treatments they should agree to, or about whether their lives have become so intolerable that suicide is the best way out. But my awareness of the social nature of so-called autonomous choice makes me regard as justified *democratic* attempts to persuade my fellow citizens that laws against counselling and abetting suicide, and laws against killing of persons at their request should remain in force, to *enhance*, not diminish, the autonomy of the vulnerable.

In conclusion, I would suggest that morality is rarely a matter of a single overriding principle which can cover all situations of dilemma. The true situation is one of tension between the principles of autonomy, beneficence and justice, but this tension can result in the enrichment of all three. In bringing the principle of justice to bear on a topic often seen as merely a question of autonomy versus paternalism, I hope to add a different dimension to the current debate about whose rights are being violated.

Conclusion: an overview of
the debate

JEAN PORTER

Most people would agree that someone who is terminally ill is not obliged to prolong his life at any cost whatever, and a physician in charge of such a patient is not obliged to go to any lengths to preserve her patient's life. Moreover, there is general agreement that a physician may take drastic steps to relieve the suffering of a moribund patient, even when these will also hasten his death. What, then, is to prevent the physician from taking actions aimed directly and immediately at ending her patient's life, if that is the only way to free him from intractable suffering?

Until recently, the answer to this question would have seemed clear to most people (at least in theory). Such a course of action is ruled out because it would be murder. For many, this is still the only thing that needs to be said on the subject. But for many others, perhaps now a majority, matters are no longer so clear-cut. As Robin Gill documents, there has been a significant increase in support for euthanasia among both churchgoers and society as a whole in Great Britain, and while I am not aware of comparable statistics for the United States, support for the practice seems to be growing there as well.[1]

It is apparent that we are in the midst of a significant shift of opinion with respect to euthanasia. It is perhaps too early to say how deep this change is, but it has already had social and legal effects in Europe and the United States which will not easily be reversed.

How should the Christian respond to these developments? The twelve essays in this volume offer us thoughtful responses to this question. While they do not cover every possible argument on the question of euthanasia which might be advanced from within a Christian theological context, they do illustrate the main lines of approach.

In what follows, I will offer an overview of the issues raised by euthanasia, seen from within the context of Christian theological ethics. In doing so, I will take the essays by Professors Gill, Badham and Campbell as my primary points of reference, without however attempting to address each of the issues that they raise. My main purpose is to clarify the central issues in the debate over euthanasia, and not to argue for my own positions. At the same time, it seems artificial (not to say coy) to avoid any reference to my own views on these issues, and I have not attempted to do so.

Killing, murder, and euthanasia: situating the argument

The growing public acceptance of euthanasia through much of the industrialized world seems to some to reflect a breakdown in moral consensus, or even, in the words of the papal encyclical *Evangelium Vitae*, a dominant 'culture of death', to which the only appropriate Christian responses are condemnation and opposition, or withdrawal.[2] This reaction is understandable. After all, euthanasia involves killing a human being, whatever else we may say about it. If we as a society are prepared to consider this as anything other than murder, surely our moral convictions have undergone a sea change. Or have they?

It is not clear that this is so. The fact is, few in our society, Christian or otherwise, would be prepared to say that any and every act of killing a human being is morally tantamount to murder.[3] There is a widespread (albeit not universal) consensus that it is sometimes permissible to kill in wartime or in self-defence, and many would also admit the legitimacy of capital punishment or abortion. Euthanasia cannot be assimilated to any of these other forms of killing, but the fact that we do not always condemn killing implies that the legitimacy of euthanasia can at least be considered within the framework of our common morality.

Moreover, the prohibition against murder is not an arbitrary enactment, like the rule that drivers in Great Britain should keep to the left. It has a point, or rather, multiple points, in terms of which it should be understood and applied to specific cases. We prohibit murder because, ordinarily, death is one of the worst misfortunes that can befall a person. For this reason, persons usually prefer to stay alive, and so murder adds the violation of autonomy to its more obvious harm. Moreover, the murderer places herself in a position of an arbiter of life and death in relation to another human being and, by doing so, she violates the fundamental equality which exists, or should exist, among all human beings. Finally, most persons feel that human life has an intrinsic value, in virtue of which the loss of a human life is always a matter for regret, and killing should be justified, if at all, only for the most exigent of reasons.[4]

This analysis of the rationale for the prohibition against murder is not meant to be exhaustive. None the less, it does cast some light on the question why some forms of killing are generally considered to be permissible, while most are not. That is, when we examine permissible forms of killing, we find that they characteristically occur in cases in which one or more of the main reasons for prohibiting killing is absent. In the case of killing in wartime or in capital punishment, the act of killing is considered to be carried out by and on behalf of the community, acting through its designated representatives, and for this reason, the acts in question do not seem to undermine fundamental equality among individual persons.[5] Significantly, some forms of killing in wartime contexts *are* considered to be murder, for example, the killing of defenceless prisoners; it would also be murder for someone other than a duly appointed executioner to kill someone under sentence of death. In the case of abortion, on the other hand, the human being which is killed has never attained self-awareness, and therefore does not experience death as a loss. The case of killing in self-defence is somewhat anomalous, since it is the act of a private individual, and is directed against someone who presumably would prefer to go on living. In this case, however, we consider the responsibility for the killing to be shifted, so to speak, to the aggressor who provokes it by his own attack.

To prevent misunderstanding, I should add that I am not here defending any of these kinds of killing. For each of them, it would be possible to argue that in spite of the fact that some of the reasons for prohibiting killing do not apply, other and weightier reasons for prohibiting killing still do obtain. My point is simply that killing in wartime, capital punishment, abortion, and killing in self-defence are all plausibly defensible in terms of the rationale for the prohibition against murder, and that is why none of them can be judged straightaway to be forms of murder.

Euthanasia raises difficulties, I would suggest, because it also characteristically occurs in cases in which some of the reasons for prohibiting murder do not apply. Someone who is near death and who is suffering considerable pain, physically or mentally, as a result of his illness, may well consider that life has little or no value for him, whatever value it may have in the abstract. The same may be true of someone whose life is so gravely impaired that she is incapable of satisfactions and attainments which are centrally important to her. In such circumstances, it may appear that we would not be harming a person significantly, and might even be conferring a benefit, by killing him. Moreover, if someone actively wants to die, then killing is not a violation of her will to stay alive, and in the case of someone who is irreversibly comatose, or who has never been sentient, the individual has no will against which we may be said to act.

None of these considerations weighs conclusively in favour of the licitness of euthanasia. Other, very serious reasons for prohibiting killing still obtain in the kinds of cases sketched above; it would still be a violation of the equality which obtains between individuals within a community, and it is at the very least in tension with a fundamental stance of reverence for human life. In my own view, these considerations are not only weighty, but decisive.

Nonetheless, it is important to realize that a case can be made for euthanasia without necessarily rejecting the more fundamental conviction that murder is wrong. While that case is not finally convincing (as I believe), the fact remains that it can be made, plausibly and in good faith, by men and women who share the same fundamental moral convictions as the rest of us. Moreover, as Professor Gill documents, the debate over euthanasia cannot be cast in terms of secular advocates versus Christian protesters.[6]

For these reasons, the violently negative comments of some Christian theologians and church leaders, exemplified by *Evangelium Vitae*'s view of the debate over euthanasia as symptomatic of a 'culture of death', appear to me to be unhelpful. Not only is it the case that serious moral concerns motivate those on both sides of the euthanasia debate but, to a considerable degree, they share the same concerns. Unless we can acknowledge this, the euthanasia debate will run into the same kind of acrimonious stalemate as the debate over abortion has done.

Two preliminary issues: suicide, and the acting/allowing distinction

There is some tendency to discuss suicide and euthanasia as if they raised more or less the same issues, a tendency reinforced by the common practice of speaking of 'assisted suicide' as if it were a synonym for euthanasia. In my view, this tendency should be resisted; suicide and euthanasia raise different issues, if only because there is an irreducible difference between doing something to oneself, and doing the same thing to another person.

At the same time, the issues of suicide and euthanasia cannot be separated, particularly for the Christian theologian. If I am not justified in ending my own life, even to cut short a painful, prolonged dying, it is difficult to see how someone else could be justified in ending my life for me. For this reason, the traditional Christian prohibition of suicide taken by itself would appear to rule out euthanasia as well.

Suicide has traditionally been assimilated to murder within the

Christian tradition (in spite of the fact that suicide by definition does not involve killing someone against his will), on the grounds that the suicide usurps God's authority over life and death. Additionally, suicide is sometimes seen as a refusal of God's providential care, a way of closing oneself to the values, even the unexpected joys, which can come into even the most wretched life. These arguments sound very different in tone, but in practice they reinforce each other, since a stance of trust in providence implies an attitude of respectful openness to the guidance of a higher power—an authority, in other words.

It is at this point that Paul Badham locates one of his main arguments for the legitimacy of both suicide and euthanasia.[7] In his view, the Christian prohibition against suicide and euthanasia reflects an attitude towards providence which is now outmoded. There was a time, he claims, when Christians condemned the practice of medicine on the grounds that it is a form of rebellion against God's providential will. Today, because we do not view sickness as a visitation from God, we acknowledge the legitimacy of medical care. By the same token, he argues, we should also let go of the prohibitions against suicide and euthanasia, since these reflect the same archaic view of our responsibilities in the face of God's providence.

Professor Badham relies in part on a false premiss. It is not the case that Christianity once condemned medical practice wholesale, even though specific practices have been condemned, sometimes for very dubious reasons.[8] Beginning in the patristic era, Christian communities founded and supported hospitals; the formal teaching of medicine in the Christian West began in Salerno in about 1100; human dissection received official church sanction in 1482, but this practice had been going on for some time previously.

None the less, Professor Badham raises an important issue. It is not self-evident that respect for God's providence necessarily rules out taking positive actions to influence the course of events. To the contrary, Christians throughout the centuries have combined a belief in God's providence with a commitment to vigorous action, and failure to act on one's behalf, relying on providence, has traditionally been condemned as tempting God. Why, then, should we draw the line at suicide?

The answer, I would suggest, lies in the fact that death is qualitatively different from anything else that can befall a human being. So long as we live, whatever happens to us and whatever we do, there is still some space in which God's providence can work. Death closes our future in time and, for this reason, it forecloses further possibilities for change, spiritual healing, and response to God's invitation; or at least, it does so if it is true, as I believe, that our fundamental identity can only be shaped in time. For this reason, someone who chooses to end his own life is taking on a tremendous responsibility, to say the least, and perhaps it is a responsibility which no one should assume.[9]

At the same time, suicide carries with it an ambiguity which prevents sure judgement on either side of the question. We find it difficult to respond to even the most seemingly justified suicide with wholehearted admiration, and yet we cannot easily condemn even the most apparently gratuitous act of self-destruction. What are we to make of this ambiguity? There is a clue in the scholastic view that suicide is wrong because it is unnatural. There does indeed seem to be something unnatural, a violation of a fundamental human tendency towards wellbeing and life, in even the most understandable act of suicide. A person must be under very great pressure indeed in order to act against this most basic of inclinations. This does not necessarily mean that suicide is always wrong, but it does indicate that it is an act of desperation. We find it difficult to share in the thoughts and feelings of someone who is suicidal; we do not know what we ourselves would do in a similar situation. It is difficult to know how to formulate moral judgements in the face of such extremities. Morality has its limits, and perhaps this is one of them.

Professor Badham raises another question which is also central for Alastair Campbell. Is there a morally significant difference between withholding or withdrawing life-saving medical treatment, thus allowing someone to die, and killing him outright? In Professor Badham's view, the distinction between killing and allowing to die is arbitrary; for Professor Campbell, to the contrary, this distinction is necessary if we are to preserve the delicate balance between respect for life and compassion for the dying which forms the 'moral context of medical care'.[10] Clearly, this question goes to the heart of the euthanasia debate. If there is no real difference between allowing someone to die, and killing him outright, it is difficult to see how the prohibition against euthanasia can be sustained.

The distinction between acting to bring about a result and allowing the same result to take place should not be confused with the distinction between direct and indirect intention or causality, which arises from the traditional doctrine of double effect. On this latter view, an action which has two effects, one good and the other bad, may be permitted if the bad effect is neither caused by the good effect, nor intended as such by the agent. The classical example in medical contexts is provided by the doctor who gives a terminally ill patient a very strong painkiller, foreseeing but not intending that this will also bring about his death. However, this doctrine generates issues similar to the acting/allowing distinction, since it too implies that acts cannot be evaluated solely in terms of their final outcomes.

The exchanges between Professors Badham and Campbell and their respondents offer a good illustration of the ways in which the acting/allowing distinction and the doctrine of double effect figure in the euthanasia debate. Space does not permit even a cursory effort to sort out these issues here; however, for the record, I agree with Professor Campbell. Even though it is analytically problematic, the acting/allowing distinction seems to me to be too fundamental to our moral intuitions in a wide range of cases to be abandoned as both Professor Badham and (in a different way) Dr Richmond suggest.

Justice, autonomy, and the social good

It is sometimes said that euthanasia should not be legalized because to do so will have undesirable social effects, for example by putting pressure on some individuals to allow themselves to be killed in order not to place burdens on others. Arguments along these lines are usually referred to as 'slippery slope' arguments although, as Professor Gill points out, this label can be misleading.[11] At any rate, he and Professor Campbell offer two versions of this general argument, as does Helen Oppenheimer in her response to Professor Badham.

After summarizing the social changes since the legalization of divorce and abortion in Great Britain, Professor Gill warns that if we legalize euthanasia, we will find ourselves faced with a similar sea change in social practices and attitudes. More specifically, he raises the possibility that the practice of euthanasia will lead to a 'procedural deterioration' through which a limited right will expand far beyond the limits originally foreseen, just as has happened with respect to both abortion and divorce.

It may seem that Professor Gill's argument begs important questions. If we consider divorce and abortion to be morally justifiable, why should we care about their increased incidence? By the same token, why should we be alarmed at the prospect of a rise in the incidence of euthanasia?

As Professor Gill would perhaps respond, matters are more complex than this question suggests. While most people would agree that divorce and abortion are sometimes justifiable, almost no one would view either as a cause for celebration. Both involve tragic choices which should never be undertaken lightly, and many who support the legitimacy of both options would also agree that society has a legitimate interest in discouraging their widespread use. For all these reasons, there is no inconsistency in regretting the greatly increased incidence of a justifiable practice. I do not mean to suggest that Professor Gill himself considers euthanasia to be justifiable, but only to point out that even a supporter of the practice might logically share his worry about procedural deterioration.

In addition, the legalization of euthanasia carries with it the danger that some individuals who would prefer to live will be pressured into accepting death, a concern shared by Professor

Campbell, Lady Oppenheimer, and Dr Biggar.[12] Professor Badham remarks at one point that legalizing abortion has not resulted in anyone being forced to have an abortion against her will.[13] While this is probably true, strictly speaking, it is also true that the legalization of abortion has made it far easier to pressure women into having abortions that they are reluctant to undergo, and it has also made it easier for others (the father, the woman's family) to refuse support for the child to be. These are precisely the kinds of social pressures which worry many opponents of euthanasia.

This brings us to Professor Campbell's claim that legalizing euthanasia would be a violation of the principle of justice, on the grounds that to do so would upset the delicate balance of sensibilities and concerns which currently inform medical care for the gravely ill and the dying. As matters now stand, he argues, we are forced by both our moral commitments and the law to attempt to hold together a compassionate concern to alleviate suffering as far as possible, with a vigilant respect for human life. If this balance were upset, the commitment to protect fragile human life would be dangerously eroded, and vulnerable persons would find themselves pressured to allow themselves to be killed. For this reason, as Professor Campbell remarks in his response to comments, our current laws against euthanasia actually enhance the autonomy of the most vulnerably ill, and it would be an injustice to repeal them.[14]

This seems to imply that euthanasia should be prohibited because of the probable effects of legalizing it. However, if I have understood him correctly, Professor Campbell's argument does not turn on an assessment of the consequences of euthanasia, if 'consequences' is to be understood in a purely utilitarian way. Rather, he is insisting that euthanasia must be evaluated as a social practice which conveys a set of attitudes and expectations. Seen from this perspective, even seemingly justified acts of euthanasia can be seen to undermine a balancing of concerns which protects the most vulnerable members of society. Although Professor Campbell does not invoke this particular principle, his argument suggests that Christians should oppose euthanasia as an expression of the 'fundamental option for the poor'.[15]

Professor Campbell does not quite say that there is something intrinsically wrong with euthanasia *per se*, but his argument seems to me to imply as much. (Or perhaps I read him in this way because it is congruent with my own view.) Given the social context within which all our actions take place, an act of euthanasia intrinsically expresses a stance towards others which at best gives too much weight to compassion, and too little to a vigilant respect for life. In addition, and as a result of the kind of action that euthanasia itself is, it will predictably have the further effect of undermining this balance in other contexts.

I would add one further point, without pretending to argue for it here. In my view, euthanasia is morally wrong because it is a violation of the equality which exists between one person and another. This seems to me to be a decisive consideration, because respect for equality is fundamental to our concept of morality itself. For this reason, I would argue, no individual person should claim authority over the life of another, *even if* that other asks to be killed.[16]

This brings us to the question of autonomy, which looms large in these essays as it does in the wider debate over euthanasia. Both suicide and euthanasia are often defended on the grounds that the right to make choices about one's own life includes, critically, the right to choose to end that life. By denying people the right to make such a choice, it is said, we are guilty of paternalism, that is to say, of limiting the freedom of others in the name of protecting them from themselves.

In contrast, it is sometimes said that autonomy is antithetical to Christians, because we are committed to recognizing that we do not belong to ourselves, we belong to God. This latter claim is certainly true, and yet it is difficult to see why it implies a rejection of autonomy as a value. After all, no one is better placed to discern what God is calling an individual to be and to do than the individual herself, and she cannot respond to God's call in her life without some degree of personal freedom. It is an open question how far this freedom should extend, and I do not mean to suggest that it necessarily includes a freedom to die or to procure one's own

death; but it does not seem to me that a blanket rejection of autonomy as a value is a theologically sound way of dealing with the
problems of suicide and euthanasia. On this point, I generally
agree with Professor Badham.

In his response to Professor Campbell, Nigel Biggar raises a more
telling objection to the appeal to autonomy. He reminds us that
human freedom does not emerge in a vacuum; what we want is
shaped by society's expectations, and may actually be antithetical
to our best interests overall. For this reason, he suggests, respect for
autonomy may sometimes be tantamount to 'an act of indifference—even of abandonment'.[17] This line of argument is reminis-
cent of the claims of some feminists that the self-sacrificial desires
of many women should be evaluated in the context of a society
which inculcates such desires in women from their earliest childhood. In my view, there is a great deal to be said for this line of
argument, although it raises issues which cannot be pursued here.

At any rate, it seems to me that here are limits to what one individual can ask another to do, even in the name of autonomy. We
come up against one such limit here; that is, I do not have a right
to ask someone to kill me, nor should I accede to such a request
from another.

This is likely to seem unsatisfactory to many; it does not seem
fully satisfactory even to me. It is all too easy to imagine a situation
so painful and desperate that in spite of all that can be said to the
contrary, a merciful killing seems like the only humane response,
as for example in the case of a soldier injured on the battlefield, suffering horribly, and with no hope of attaining even palliative medical care. I myself would still hesitate to say that it would be right
to kill in such a case, but I would also be more than reluctant to
judge another, or to try to predict what I would do myself.
Euthanasia is one of those issues which we can probably never
resolve to our complete satisfaction, and perhaps we should worry
if we think we have done so.

This may seem to support legalization, but I do not think so. In
the United States, at any rate, the legal situation as it currently
stands in most states seems to reflect the difficulties and ambigu-

ities generated by the practice of euthanasia. The practice is out-
lawed, thus reflecting a social consensus that it is wrong, and presumably discouraging it; but at the same time, no one was actually
convicted of any crime in a case of euthanasia up until 1976.[18]
Perhaps this is the best that can be done at a social level in address-
ing this complex question. At any rate, I would agree with both
Professor Gill and Professor Campbell that the risks of legalizing
euthanasia far outweigh any possible benefits.[19]

Notes

1. Robin Gill, 'The challenge of euthanasia', pp. 19–22. Even though it
    is already slightly dated, Roger Dworkin's *Limits: The Role of the Law
    in Bioethical Decision Making* (Bloomington, IN: Indiana University
    Press, 1996), pp. 109–46 offers an excellent discussion of the cur-
    rent state of the law and social attitudes in the United States as they
    pertain to euthanasia.
2. Pope John Paul II, *The Gospel of Life* (*Evangelium Vitae*) (New York:
    Random House, 1995), para. 12, p. 22; para. 28, p. 50.
3. Contrary to what Julie Norris suggests, the Roman Catholic Church
    does not teach (in *Evangelium Vitae* or elsewhere) that human life is
    so sacred that it can never be attacked under any circumstances
    whatever. Rather, the official Catholic view is that *innocent* human
    life can never be taken, but killing in wartime and capital punish-
    ment are sometimes morally licit, albeit only under narrowly defined
    circumstances.
4. As Ronald Dworkin powerfully argues in his *Life's Dominion: An
    Argument About Abortion, Euthanasia, and Individual Freedom* (New
    York: Knopf, 1993), this attitude is by no means limited to religious
    believers.
5. I believe Professor Gill is mistaken to claim that on the logic of
    Augustine's arguments, euthanasia would be morally justified if it
    were legal, because it would then be authorized by the state. Killing
    by human authority is only justified on Augustine's view if it is
    carried out *on behalf of* the community by its designated representa-
    tives, as happens in wartime or capital punishment; it is worth
    noting that he does not believe that killing in self-defence is justified
    even though he acknowledges that this practice too is legal. By the
    same token, I would argue that even if euthanasia were legalized, it
    would still be a violation of the fundamental equality between

individuals within a community, in contrast to an act of killing carried out on behalf of the community as a whole.

6. 'The challenge of euthanasia', pp. 19–22.

7. Paul Badham, 'Should Christians accept the validity of voluntary euthanasia?', pp. 48–9.

8. Apart from two brief references in Galatians and the *Didache*, Professor Badham's only evidence for the claim that Christians condemned the practice of medicine comes from A. White's *History of the Warfare of Science with Theology*, first published in 1896. This book is described by Roger French and Andrew Cunningham as a 'propagandist' work aimed at showing that the Catholic Church has always been an enemy of free thought (*Before Science: The Invention of the Friars' Natural Philosophy*, Aldershot, Hants: Scolar Press, 1996, p. 274). The medical historian Roy Porter offers a more recent and more reliable account of early Christian attitudes and practices; see his *The Greatest Benefit to Mankind: A Medical History of Humanity from Antiquity to the Present* (San Francisco: HarperCollins, 1997), pp. 83–92, 106–34, on which I rely for the remainder of this paragraph.

9. For the record, I am more inclined to accept the traditional argument that suicide is a usurpation of God's prerogatives than I once was; see my *Moral Action and Christian Ethics* (Cambridge: Cambridge University Press, 1995), pp. 115–18. At the same time, I still have the same concern about the possible misuse of this argument as I express there.

10. Badham, p. 53; Alastair Campbell, 'Euthanasia and the principle of justice', p. 87.

11. Robin Gill, 'Reply', p. 38.

12. This worry is central to Professor Campbell's essay; in addition, see Helen Oppenheimer, 'Response to Paul Badham', p. 63, and Nigel Biggar, 'Response to Alastair Campbell', p. 110.

13. Badham, p. 55; he quotes Margaret Otlowski with approval at this point.

14. Alastair Campbell, 'Reply', p. 118.

15. I am encouraged in my reading of Professor Campbell's essay by Nigel Biggar's interpretation, and Professor Campbell's response to him.

16. I argue this in more detail in *Moral Action and Christian Ethics*, pp. 113–16.

17. Biggar, p. 111.

18. Roger B. Dworkin, *Limits*, p. 113. Dworkin does not say whether there was such a conviction in 1976, or the data simply run out at

that point. At any rate, the experiences of the hapless prosecutors of Dr Jack Kevorkian make it clear that US juries are still reluctant to convict those accused in connection with an act of euthanasia.

19. I would like to thank Joseph Blenkinsopp for his comments on an earlier draft of this paper. In addition, my work on this paper was supported by grants from the Graduate School of the University of Notre Dame and the Association of Theological Schools in the United States and Canada, and I wish to express my appreciation for their support.

Index